The Mix of Military and Civilian Faculty at the United States Air Force Academy

Finding a Sustainable Balance for Enduring Success

Kirsten M. Keller, Nelson Lim, Lisa M. Harrington,
Kevin O'Neill, Abigail Haddad

Prepared for the United States Air Force
Approved for public release; distribution unlimited

RAND PROJECT AIR FORCE

The research described in this report was sponsored by the United States Air Force under Contract FA7014-06-C-0001. Further information may be obtained from the Strategic Planning Division, Directorate of Plans, Hq USAF.

Library of Congress Cataloging-in-Publication Data is available for this publication.

ISBN: 978-0-8330-7693-9

Cover image courtesy of U.S. Air Force/Mike Kaplan.

Published 2013 by the RAND Corporation
1776 Main Street, P.O. Box 2138, Santa Monica, CA 90407-2138
1200 South Hayes Street, Arlington, VA 22202-5050
4570 Fifth Avenue, Suite 600, Pittsburgh, PA 15213-2665
RAND URL: http://www.rand.org/
To order RAND documents or to obtain additional information, contact
Distribution Services: Telephone: (310) 451-7002;
Fax: (310) 451-6915; Email: order@rand.org

Preface

Since civilians were formally incorporated onto the faculty at the United States Air Force Academy (USAFA) in the early 1990s, there has been continued debate over the best mix of military and civilian faculty needed to achieve the Academy's mission. Furthermore, the Air Force currently faces difficulty in meeting USAFA faculty requirements for officers with advanced academic degrees, often resulting in understaffed departments. Funding for temporary faculty to fill these positions is also declining. This report documents research designed to address these issues by examining how potential changes to the current academic faculty composition would affect five areas of importance to USAFA's mission and to the broader U.S. Air Force: (1) cadets' officership development, (2) cadets' academic development, (3) cost, (4) staffing challenges, and (5) officer career development. The report then makes recommendations for a faculty composition that best balances these key factors and is sustainable into the future.

The research reported here was sponsored by the Assistant Secretary of the Air Force for Manpower and Reserve Affairs (SAF/MR) and the Director, Force Development, Deputy Chief of Staff for Manpower and Personnel, Headquarters U.S. Air Force (AF/A1D), and was conducted within the Manpower, Personnel, and Training Program of RAND Project AIR FORCE. The study commenced in August 2010 and continued as a subtask ("U.S. Air Force Academy Faculty Mix") of the fiscal year 2011 project "Enhancing Force Management and Development." This report should be of interest to Air Force leadership and staff, military service academies, and interested members of the general public.

RAND Project AIR FORCE

RAND Project AIR FORCE (PAF), a division of the RAND Corporation, is the U.S. Air Force's federally funded research and development center for studies and analyses. PAF provides the Air Force with independent analyses of policy alternatives affecting the development, employment, combat readiness, and support of current and future air, space, and cyber forces. Research is conducted in four programs: Force Modernization and Employment; Manpower, Personnel, and Training; Resource Management; and Strategy and Doctrine.

Additional information about PAF is available on our website:
http://www.rand.org/paf

Contents

APPENDIXES

Figures

Tables

Summary

The mission of the United States Air Force Academy (USAFA) is "to educate, train and inspire men and women to become officers of character, motivated to lead the United States Air Force in service to our nation."[1] To achieve this mission, USAFA provides cadets (roughly 4,500 students) with military training as well as a four-year college education similar to that offered at other civilian institutions.[2] Military training is overseen by the Commandant of Cadets (who holds the rank of brigadier general) and a staff of roughly 300, while academic instruction is overseen by the Dean of Faculty (who holds the rank of brigadier general) and an academic faculty of close to 600. Unlike at civilian institutions, USAFA academic classes are taught by a mix of active-duty military officers and civilian professors. At the time of this research, USAFA was authorized for 570 academic faculty members, with a mix of 71 percent military and 29 percent civilian. However, taking into account all temporary faculty members, the actual composition was closer to 37 percent civilian during the 2011 spring semester, when this research was conducted.

Initially, the USAFA academic faculty was composed of active-duty military officers only. Civilians were formally incorporated in the early 1990s, composing up to roughly 25 percent of the faculty, at the urging of Congress in response to concerns over the highly rota-

1 U.S. Air Force Academy, *The United States Air Force Academy Outcomes*, Colo., 2009.

2 USAFA is an undergraduate-only institution.

tional nature of military faculty and a lack of doctoral degrees.[3] Since that time, the debate over the best mix of military and civilian faculty to achieve the Academy's mission has continued, with USAFA's current senior leaders preferring to maintain a majority-military faculty. However, the Air Force currently faces difficulty in meeting USAFA military faculty requirements for officers with advanced academic degrees, often resulting in understaffed departments.

This report attempts to address these issues by strategically examining and providing recommendations for an academic faculty composition that balances key factors and is sustainable into the future. Specifically, it examines how general shifts in the current authorized academic faculty composition would affect five key factors of importance to both USAFA's mission and the broader U.S. Air Force:

1. *cadets' officership development:* the extent to which cadets are socialized into the Air Force culture and the role of being an officer
2. *cadets' academic development:* the extent to which cadets are provided a rigorous and intellectually challenging education
3. *cost:* the cost to the government of employing military officers compared with employing civilians as faculty members
4. *staffing challenges:* the ability to meet academic faculty staffing requirements
5. *officer career development:* the impact of USAFA instructor duty on the professional development of officers who are sent to teach.

This research draws on information from a wide range of sources, including interviews with senior leaders at USAFA, faculty focus groups, a survey of cadets, data on relative teaching effectiveness, information on faculty costs, and administrative personnel data.

---

[3] Military faculty members serve in three- to four-year teaching tours.

Cadets' Officership Development

The first factor we examined was cadets' officership development. Findings from our interviews with USAFA senior leaders and focus groups with current faculty indicate that military faculty members play a key role in cadets' officership development; they serve as role models, bring operational experience to the classroom, and provide career advice. Results from a cadet survey further support this distinction in faculty roles. Although differences were often small, cadets rated military faculty members as having a greater influence than civilian faculty on aspects of their officer development.

Cadets' Academic Development

In terms of cadets' academic development, we were not able to find conclusive evidence of differences in teaching effectiveness across faculty types. The cadet survey results also showed only minimal differences in how cadets perceive the influence of faculty groups on their intellectual skill development and the extent to which different faculty groups bring greater academic depth of knowledge to the classroom. However, findings from our interviews with USAFA senior leaders and focus groups with current faculty indicate that civilian faculty members play a key academic role at USAFA that military faculty members are not able to fill in the same way; they provide academic expertise, teaching experience, and a connection to the broader academic and research communities. The majority of civilian faculty members also hold doctorates, have greater teaching experience, and tend to hold higher academic ranks than military faculty.

Cost

We examined the average annual cost to the government of employing military officers and civilians as faculty members. The costs used for this analysis included both direct compensation paid to the military or civilian faculty member and indirect compensation costs incurred by the government, such as retirement accrual, health insurance, and relocation expenses. We also included the cost of obtaining an advanced academic degree for military officers, given that a majority of military faculty members were sponsored by USAFA to obtain their advanced academic degree to be qualified to teach. When comparing the relative cost to the government of employing a military or civilian faculty member, our calculations show that, on average, the least costly military faculty member (captain/O-3 direct hire with no Air Force–funded degree) is more expensive than a civilian instructor, assistant professor, or associate professor. If an Air Force officer (irrespective of grade) is sent for any Air Force–funded degree (master's or doctorate), he or she is, on average, more costly than a civilian faculty member at the highest academic rank (professor).

Staffing Challenges

Currently, the Air Force faces difficulty in meeting USAFA's staffing requirements for military faculty. This is due to several different factors, including a lack of officers with the necessary advanced academic degrees, staffing allocation plans that prioritize other billets over USAFA, and misalignment with career paths, and deployments. Further, due to budget limitations, funding for temporary faculty to fill empty positions is also being reduced.

Officer Career Development

Finally, our analysis of the impact of USAFA instructor duty on officer career development indicates that faculty tours at USAFA do not always fit designated career paths and result in missed opportunities to gain operational and command experience compared with nonfaculty peers. This is particularly true when officers obtain both a master's degree and doctorate and complete two payback teaching tours at USAFA. Consistent with this finding, promotion analyses indicated that those who taught at USAFA only as company-grade officers had better overall advancement rates to higher pay grades than officers who taught at USAFA as field-grade officers only or officers who taught as both company-grade and field-grade officers. This suggests that it is better for officers to teach at USAFA early in their careers as company-grade officers. However, there is a misalignment in manpower grade authorizations and assignments at USAFA, with company-grade officers currently understaffed and lieutenant colonels/O-5s overstaffed. Company-grade officers are not understaffed across the Air Force, however. Instead, challenges related to the timing of degrees, career paths, and different staffing prioritizations contribute to the misalignment at USAFA. Practices leading to this misalignment in manpower grade authorizations and assignments must be addressed to avoid a negative impact on officer career development.

Conclusion and Policy Recommendations

Table S.1 lists five potential staffing options reflecting general shifts in the percentage of authorized military and civilian faculty positions and the current misalignment in manpower authorizations and assignments. We examined the impact that each of these shifts would have on the five factors presented earlier, compared with maintaining current faculty authorizations. As the table shows, although keeping the current authorized percentages of military and civilian faculty members would have a neutral impact across all factors, this option is not sustainable and is undesirable for USAFA. It would perpetuate the staffing challenges USAFA currently faces in finding military officers with the appropriate advanced academic degrees, as well as the staffing practices that negatively affect officer career development. Looking across the other options, increasing civilian representation has a positive impact across many factors, and working to fill current company-grade authorizations will help officer career development.

Table S.1
Impact of Staffing Options on Five Key Factors

Staffing Options	Cadets' Officership Development	Cadets' Academic Development	Cost	Staffing Challenges	Officer Career Development
Keep current military-civilian ratio					
Keep current military-civilian ratio; fill company-grade authorizations					
Increase % of military faculty					
Increase % of civilian faculty					
Increase % of civilian faculty; fill company-grade authorizations					

Unsustainable | Negative impact | Potential negative impact | Neutral | Potential positive impact | Positive impact

Based on this analysis, we developed the following four recommendations. It is important to note that we treated all factors equally in developing our recommendations. The Air Force will ultimately need to make strategic decisions regarding which factors are the highest priorities.

Recommendation 1: A shift toward greater civilian representation is advisable unless its potential negative impact on building cadet officership outweighs the other factors. As illustrated in Table S.1, increasing the authorized percentage of civilian faculty would have a positive impact across many factors. Despite the potential negative impact on cadets' officership development, cost and staffing challenges would be reduced, and there is a potential positive impact on academics, assuming that high-quality civilians are hired. Our analysis did not point to any silver-bullet ratio of military to civilian faculty.

However, if the Air Force chooses to shift toward greater civilian representation, one option that should have little negative impact is to gradually increase civilian representation to roughly 40 percent of the authorized positions, reflecting current faculty operating conditions at the time of our research when including all temporary faculty (roughly 37 percent civilian in total).

Recommendation 2: The mix of military and civilian faculty should vary across departments, with military representation concentrated in academic disciplines that are needed elsewhere in the Air Force. Finding military faculty with the appropriate advanced academic degrees to teach in academic departments that are not directly aligned with an Air Force specialty or highly utilized in the broader Air Force (e.g., philosophy, history) is very challenging. Therefore, we do not recommend a one-size-fits-all ratio across departments. This approach would also help provide better payback for the costs of Air Force–sponsored advanced academic degrees.

Recommendation 3: Align military faculty assignments with manpower grade authorizations by filling current authorizations for company-grade officers. Our research indicates that having been an instructor at USAFA early in one's career is less likely to hinder the career development of officers. Thus, it is important for officers who teach at USAFA to do so early in their careers. Of course, there may be initial challenges to achieving this realignment, including coordination between the Air Force Personnel Center and USAFA and ensuring that officers are obtaining their advanced academic degrees early enough to have the opportunity to fulfill instructor duty while they are junior officers.

Recommendation 4: The Air Force should monitor and assess the impact of any changes to the current military and civilian faculty mix on USAFA's ability to fulfill its mission. As USAFA implements changes to the composition of its faculty, it will be important to monitor any potentially negative effects on the factors examined as part of this research, the key outcomes identified by USAFA as part of its strategic plan, and the overall ability of USAFA to fulfill its mission.

In conclusion, when holding all factors equal, we believe that a shift in the faculty ratio toward greater civilian representation will not be harmful to USAFA but will instead have the most positive impact. Taken together, we believe that these recommendations will result in a USAFA faculty that is better able to help the Academy meet its mission and is more sustainable into the future.

Acknowledgments

We are grateful to the many people who were involved in this research. In particular, we would like to thank our U.S. Air Force sponsors, Daniel Sitterly, then Director, Force Development, Office of the Deputy Chief of Staff for Manpower and Personnel (AF/A1D), and Daniel Ginsberg, Assistant Secretary of the Air Force for Manpower and Reserve Affairs (SAF/MR), as well as Lt Gen Darrell Jones, Deputy Chief of Staff for Manpower, Personnel, and Services (AF/A1). We would also like to thank our key points of contact in those offices for their help and guidance throughout this study: Bill Booth, then Deputy Assistant Secretary of the Air Force for Force Management Integration (SAF/MRM); Col (ret.) William Hampton, Commissioning Programs Division (AF/A1DO); Dave French (then in SAF/MRM), Thomas Shubert (SAF/MRM), and Lt Col Tammy Trychon (AF/A1DO).

We also benefited from the contributions of the many USAFA staff and faculty who participated in our interviews and focus groups and provided the data and background that we needed to complete this study. First, we would like to thank Lt Gen Michael Gould (Superintendent, USAFA), Brig Gen Dana Born (Dean of Faculty, USAFA), and Col Richard Fullerton (Vice Dean of Faculty, USAFA) for their cooperation and help with our research. We are also grateful to Lt Col Brian Maue (then in the Department of Management, USAFA), who served as our main point of contact for the Dean of Faculty; Col Michael Therianos (Director, Strategic Plans and Programs, Requirements, Assessments, and Analyses, USAFA), who served as our main point of contact for the Superintendent; and Kathy O'Donnell

(Senior Assessment Analyst, Assessment and Analyses Division, USAFA), who helped facilitate our research efforts at the Academy. We also thank James West (former USAFA professor of economics) for his assistance with the data and analysis regarding teaching effectiveness. We would not have been able to complete our work without his great generosity.

We thank the office of Graduate Education, Civilian Institution Programs, Air Force Institute of Technology, for providing data and process information to support the derivation of costs associated with military officers obtaining advanced academic degrees. We are also grateful to representatives from the Academic and Special Utilization Branch, Air Force Personnel Center, and the officer assignment team representatives who provided information on the military faculty assignment process at USAFA.

This report also benefited from the helpful insights and comments provided by several RAND colleagues, including Daniela Golinelli, Paul Heaton, Albert Robbert, Michael Schiefer, Perry Firoz, Paul Emslie, Kate Giglio, and Paul Steinberg. Finally, we would like to thank Michael Hansen, Catherine Augustine, and J. R. Lockwood, who provided technical reviews of this report. Their comments greatly improved the quality of this work.

Abbreviations

AD	administratively determined (a civil service pay plan)
AFIT	Air Force Institute of Technology
AFIT/CI	Air Force Institute of Technology, Civilian Institution Programs
AFPC	Air Force Personnel Center
AMT	academy military trainer
AOC	air officer commanding
DoD	U.S. Department of Defense
FY	fiscal year
GAO	U.S. General Accounting Office (now U.S. Government Accountability Office)
IPZ	in the promotion zone
OMB	Office of Management and Budget
OTS	Officer Training School
OUSD(C)	Office of the Under Secretary of Defense, Comptroller
PITO	Personal, Interpersonal, Team, and Organizational (model)

ROTC	Reserve Officer Training Corps
SGLI	Servicemembers' Group Life Insurance
STP	students, transients, patients, and prisoners
TDY	temporary duty
USAFA	United States Air Force Academy
USMA	United States Military Academy
USNA	United States Naval Academy

CHAPTER ONE

Introduction

The mission of the United States Air Force Academy (USAFA) is "to educate, train and inspire men and women to become officers of character, motivated to lead the United States Air Force in service to our nation."[1] To achieve this mission, USAFA provides cadets (roughly 4,500 students across four class years) with military training as well as a four-year college education similar to that offered at civilian institutions.[2] Military training is overseen by the Commandant of Cadets (who holds the rank of brigadier general) and a staff of roughly 300. Academic instruction is overseen by the Dean of Faculty (who holds the rank of brigadier general) and a faculty body composed of a mix of active-duty military officers and civilian professors. At the time of this research, USAFA had 570 authorized academic faculty positions, with a mix of 71 percent military and 29 percent civilian faculty members.

When USAFA was founded, the faculty was composed of active-duty military officers only. Civilians were formally incorporated onto the faculty in the early 1990s at the urging of Congress in response to concerns over the highly rotational nature of military faculty, who only serve three- to four-year teaching tours, and a lack of doctoral degrees among officers. The initial goal was for civilians to compose up to 25 percent of the academic faculty.

Since that time, there has been continued debate over the mix of military and civilian faculty needed to best achieve USAFA's mis-

---

1 U.S. Air Force Academy, *The United States Air Force Academy Outcomes*, Colo., 2009.

2 USAFA is an undergraduate-only institution.

sion.[3] Furthermore, the Academy has difficulty finding officers with the appropriate advanced academic degrees, often resulting in understaffed departments. In fact, in a recent statement, USAFA's Dean of Faculty concluded that "most of [USAFA's] challenges lie in attracting and maintaining the right mix of military faculty and arise due to competition with the operational needs of the Air Force."[4] Additionally, in today's resource-constrained environment, funding for temporary faculty to fill positions in understaffed departments is being reduced. To address these issues, the Office of the Secretary of the Air Force for Manpower and Reserve Affairs (SAF/MR) and the Air Force Directorate of Force Development (AF/A1D) asked RAND Project AIR FORCE to strategically examine and make recommendations for a USAFA academic faculty composition that would best meet the needs of the Air Force and would be sustainable into the future.

Study Objectives

In carrying out this research, our primary goal was to examine how general shifts in the current composition of military and civilian academic faculty would affect key factors of importance to both USAFA's mission and the broader U.S. Air Force. We identified five factors we considered critical to examine:

1. *cadets' officership development:* the extent to which cadets are socialized into the Air Force culture and the role of being an officer
2. *cadets' academic development:* the extent to which cadets are provided a rigorous and intellectually challenging education

---

3 See Appendix A for a detailed discussion regarding the history of the faculty composition at the U.S. service academies and USAFA in particular.

4 Brig Gen Dana H. Born, statement before the Subcommittee on Oversight and Investigations, Committee on Armed Services, U.S. House of Representatives, at the hearing "Beyond Service Core Competency: Are Our Junior Officers Prepared for Today's Security Environment?" Washington, D.C., July 15, 2009, p. 4.

3. *cost:* the cost to the government of employing military officers compared with civilians as faculty members
4. *staffing challenges:* the ability to meet academic faculty staffing requirements
5. *officer career development:* the impact of USAFA instructor duty on the professional development of officers who are sent to teach.

Analytical Approach

To assess the impact of potential shifts in the current composition of military and civilian academic faculty on these five factors, we undertook the following research tasks. First, we gathered background information on USAFA, including changes in the faculty structure over the years, and reviewed previous studies and reports on the mix of military and civilian faculty at the service academies. Next, we conducted semi-structured interviews with USAFA senior leaders to understand current institutional perspectives on the faculty composition. Following these interviews, we held focus groups with current faculty members and interviewed faculty in key leadership positions to gather information on the roles that different types of faculty play in helping USAFA achieve its mission and on potential challenges in obtaining qualified military and civilian faculty to teach at USAFA. We then administered a survey to cadets to examine whether they perceived a difference between military and civilian faculty members in terms of influence on aspects of their officer and academic development. To further assess faculty members' impact on academic development, we also statistically examined whether there were differences in the teaching effectiveness of military and civilian faculty. To establish the impact on cost to the Air Force, we examined data on the average annual cost of employing a military or civilian faculty member. We also examined data on promotion rates to explore whether USAFA instructor duty affected officers' career advancement potential.

Finally, we interviewed and gathered information from key stakeholders, including staff at the Air Force Personnel Center (AFPC) who are responsible for assigning military officers to USAFA faculty duty and staff at the Air Force Institute of Technology (AFIT) who are responsible for managing the advanced academic degree process. We also conducted interviews with the deans of faculty at the United States Military Academy (USMA) and the United States Naval Academy (USNA) to gather information on their faculty systems and compositions as a point of comparison.

Organization of This Report

The remainder of this report describes our research findings and concluding recommendations. Chapter Two presents a descriptive overview of USAFA's current faculty composition, and Chapter Three summarizes current USAFA senior leader perspectives regarding the ideal faculty mix. Chapters Four through Eight present the main research findings for each of the five factors we examined: Chapters Four and Five discuss the role of faculty in cadets' officership development and academic development, respectively; Chapter Six provides an overview of the relative cost differences between military and civilian faculty; Chapter Seven presents findings on staffing challenges; and Chapter Eight examines the impact of USAFA instructor duty on officer career development. Chapter Nine presents our conclusions and recommendations.

The report also includes five appendixes. Appendix A provides a historical overview of reports and events related to the faculty composition at USAFA. Appendix B offers additional detail on our methodology and analysis for the interviews and focus groups. Appendix C explains the methodology for the cadet survey. Appendix D provides more details on our teaching effectiveness data and analyses, and Appendix E provides an overview of how our analysis examining teaching effectiveness differs from related research.

CHAPTER TWO

Current Faculty Composition at the United States Air Force Academy

This chapter provides a descriptive overview of the current composition of academic faculty at USAFA. Here, we can see the long-term, systemic implications of previously set policies. The data presented here were provided by USAFA in March 2011.[1]

Today's USAFA Faculty

Currently, USAFA authorizations are for 570 academic faculty members with a mix of roughly 71 percent military officers and 29 percent civilians. However, if we account for military staffing shortages and temporary faculty, actual civilian representation was closer to 37 percent in the spring semester of 2011 when this research was conducted (see Figure 2.1).[2]

Compared with the faculty composition at the other service academies (USNA and USMA), USAFA's is most aligned with the USMA model. USMA tries to maintain a mix of 25 percent civilian and 75 percent military faculty. Due to similar military staffing shortages, however, USMA reported a mix that was slightly over 25 percent civil-

1 The information provided by USAFA was based on self-reported data from all faculty teaching at USAFA during the time of our research. The data were subsequently reviewed by academic department representatives and the Vice Dean of Faculty to verify their accuracy.

2 Temporary faculty members are defined as teaching faculty not serving in a permanent position overseen by the Dean of Faculty (e.g., part-time hires filling in for deployed military, one-class-per-semester instructors from other units).

Figure 2.1
Percentages of Authorized and Assigned Military and Civilian Faculty

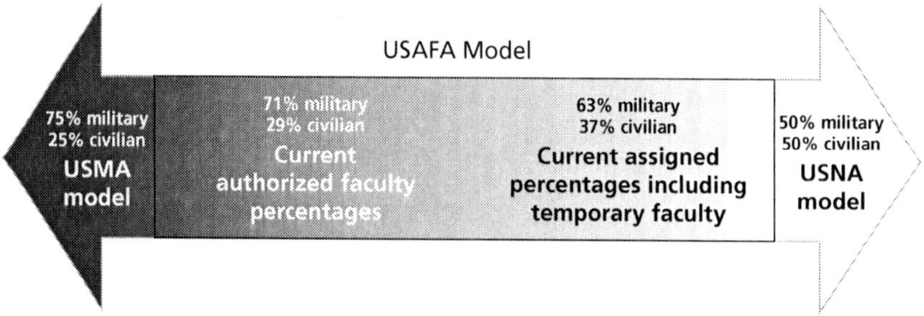

RAND *MG1237-2.1*

ian at the time of this research. On the other hand, USNA has tried to maintain a balanced 50/50 mix since its founding. USNA's current faculty mix has also been affected by staffing shortages, however, driving the actual civilian representation to more than 60 percent.[3]

Military Faculty

Generally speaking, there are three types of active-duty military teaching faculty at USAFA: permanent professors, senior military faculty, and rotational military faculty. Each of these different faculty groups serves in different roles and provides unique contributions to USAFA.

Permanent professors are assigned to USAFA to "provide continuity to academic programs, to increase stability in institutional governance through membership in Academy boards and committees, and to embody the quality standards of airman-scholar-citizen."[4] All academically qualified faculty, as well as other qualified Air Force officers at the rank of major and above, are considered viable candidates for permanent professor positions. Upon selection, each permanent professor, usually holding the rank of colonel, typically serves as the head

[3] Information on the faculty composition at USMA and USNA was obtained from interviews with each institution's dean of faculty in July 2011.

[4] HQ United States Air Force Academy Instruction 36-151, *Permanent Professor*, March 20, 2000, p. 1.

of an academic department. A dean of faculty, who holds the rank of brigadier general, is also selected from among the permanent professors who have served as department heads. Once appointed to a permanent professor position, an officer can serve in that position until he or she accumulates 30 years of total active federally commissioned service, as stipulated by Title 10 of the U.S. Code.[5]

In addition to permanent professors, a small number of senior military faculty members serve at USAFA.[6] However, USAFA Instruction 36-3520 directs that the combined size of the permanent professor and senior military faculty groups should not exceed 15 percent of the authorized USAFA faculty. As a minimum eligibility requirement for senior military faculty duty, an officer must hold a terminal degree and have three years of faculty service at USAFA or the Air University. He or she must also have served in an operational assignment or been deployed within the previous five years. Senior military faculty assignments have separate manpower designations from rotational faculty billets. As such, duty entails longer periods of service at USAFA to provide military leadership and subject-matter expertise to the academic departments. Once assigned this role, an individual can remain assigned as a senior military faculty member until he or she is terminated, promoted to colonel, or retired from active-duty military service.

Finally, rotational military faculty members make up the largest faculty group at USAFA. This group is composed of both field-grade officers (major/O-4 and lieutenant colonel/O-5) and company-grade officers (primarily captain/O-3). In many cases, these officers have been sponsored by USAFA to earn a master's degree or doctorate in a given academic field and then serve a follow-on tour as a faculty member. Officers will typically serve a three-year tour after receiving a master's degree and a four-year tour after receiving a doctorate. More than 60 percent of officers who have taught at USAFA with a doctorate had

---

[5] Air Force Instruction 36-3501, *Air Force Academy Operations*, April 28, 2008, certified current as of May 3, 2010.

[6] For more information, see HQ United States Air Force Academy Instruction 36-3520, *Senior Military Faculty*, March 31, 2010.

already completed a teaching tour at USAFA and had been selected to go on to earn a doctorate and come back a second time to instruct at USAFA in a more senior role.

The current grade distribution of military faculty members is presented in Table 2.1.

Table 2.1
Authorized and Assigned USAFA Active-Duty Military Faculty, by Grade

Military Grade	% of Authorized Military Faculty (*n* = 406)	% of Assigned Military Faculty (*n* = 378)
O-2	—	<1
O-3	55	27
O-4	24	25
O-5	14	40
O-6	7	7

NOTE: Percentages reflect all active-duty military faculty members (permanent professors, senior military faculty, and rotational faculty) but not temporary military faculty. Assigned military faculty include only teaching faculty serving in permanent positions under the purview of the USAFA Dean of Faculty at the time of this research, March 2011.

With the goal of maintaining a largely junior rotating military faculty, manpower grade authorizations designate the majority of all USAFA active-duty military faculty billets for company-grade officers (specifically, captains/O-3s). However, current staffing practices have meant that 72 percent of military faculty members are field-grade officers while only 28 percent are company-grade officers. This misalignment is due to many different factors, including the timing of receiving a degree, career paths, and assignment policies. We discuss the implications of this misalignment for officer career development in Chapter Eight.

Civilian Faculty

As stated earlier, civilians are to compose 29 percent of authorized USAFA academic faculty. However, during the 2011 spring semester, when this research was conducted, actual civilian representation was closer to 37 percent when all temporary faculty were taken into account.[7] Civilian faculty members do not have tenure but instead work under five-year renewable contracts. Despite this, turnover of civilian faculty has been very low over the years, with USAFA reporting a rate at less than 3 percent. Table 2.2 presents the current authorized and assigned percentages of civilian faculty by academic rank.[8]

Table 2.2
Authorized and Assigned USAFA Civilian Faculty, by Academic Rank

Academic Rank	% of Authorized Civilian Faculty (*n* = 164)	% of Assigned Civilian Faculty (*n* = 153)
Instructor	11	<1
Assistant professor	28	28
Associate professor	25	25
Professor	35	46
Visiting professor	12	8

NOTE: Percentages do not include faculty in temporary positions. Percentages may not sum to 100 due to rounding. Assigned civilian faculty include only teaching faculty serving in permanent positions under the purview of the USAFA Dean of Faculty at the time of this research, March 2011.

Among the civilian faculty, a distinction is often made between those faculty members with no prior military service experience and those with prior military service experience. This prior experience may be only a few years of military service or a 20-year career followed by retirement from the military. As Table 2.3 shows, close to half of civil-

---

7 USAFA reported a total of 80 temporary civilian faculty members and 25 temporary military faculty members at the time of this research.

8 Data provided by USAFA show many more authorized civilian visiting professors than were included in the data on assigned civilian faculty.

Table 2.3
USAFA Civilian Faculty with Prior Military Experience, by Service

Service Branch	% of Civilian Faculty (n = 153)
Air Force	32
Army	6
Marine Corps	1
Navy	3
Total	42

NOTE: Percentages do not include faculty in temporary positions.

ian faculty members had prior service experience in one of the military branches at the time of our study, and 32 percent had prior Air Force experience.

Several recent reviews of USAFA's faculty composition have criticized this large percentage of prior-service faculty members, arguing that it defeats congressional intent of incorporating civilian faculty who would bring diverse backgrounds and perspectives to the classroom.[9] USAFA has argued that its civilian hiring process tries not to "advantage military or disadvantage military, retired military."[10] However, the Academy argues that the former military personnel provide a beneficial balance of military experience and advanced scholarship that is not possible with purely civilian faculty.

[9] See ADM Charles R. Larson (ret.), *Study and Report Related to Permanent Professors at the United States Air Force Academy*, April 2004; U.S. House of Representatives, Committee on Armed Services, Subcommittee on Oversight and Investigations, *Another Crossroads? Professional Military Education Two Decades After the Goldwater-Nichols Act and the Skelton Panel*, transcript of a hearing before the Subcommittee on Oversight and Investigations, Committee on Armed Services, U.S. House of Representatives, Washington, D.C., April 2010.

[10] Born, 2009, p. 25.

Summary

USAFA has a current authorized mix of 71 percent military and 29 percent civilian faculty. However, due to military staffing shortages caused by deployments and challenges in finding military faculty with the appropriate advanced academic degrees, actual civilian representation is even higher—at 37 percent—when all temporary faculty members are included. Additionally, current military faculty assignments and manpower grade authorizations are not aligned, with company-grade officers understaffed and field-grade officers overstaffed. Finally, a large portion of civilian faculty members also have prior service experience.

CHAPTER THREE

USAFA Senior Leader Perspectives on the Ideal Faculty Mix

As a first step in this study, we conducted semistructured interviews with USAFA senior leaders and academic division heads (all of whom were active-duty or retired Air Force officers) to gather current institutional perspectives regarding the composition of USAFA's academic faculty. The interview questions focused primarily on the following three broad topics:[1]

- the role of different faculty types in helping USAFA achieve its mission
- the ideal military-civilian faculty mix
- challenges to achieving the ideal military-civilian faculty mix.

Qualitative Findings

Overall, all the USAFA senior leaders with whom we spoke maintained that both military and civilian faculty members play valuable but distinct roles in helping the Academy achieve its mission. They identified civilian faculty members as playing a key academic role at USAFA by providing academic expertise and bringing stability to the faculty (compared to the rotational nature of military members). In contrast, senior leaders identified military faculty members as playing a key role

[1] See Appendix B for the full interview protocol and more details on the qualitative data analysis.

in cadets' officership development by serving as role models and helping to create a military culture on campus.[2]

Despite valuing each of these roles, USAFA senior leaders also reported that they believe there is an ideal mix of military and civilian faculty that best achieves USAFA's mission to produce "officers of character." Specifically, we were told by all respondents that the ideal faculty mix is majority-military, with roughly 75 percent military and 25 percent civilian faculty. However, some respondents indicated that civilian representation as high as 30 or 35 percent might be acceptable. Overall, however, there was a consensus that a majority-military faculty was critical.

Importantly, several respondents also noted that there may be no "one-size-fits-all" solution across academic departments and that the ideal mix may vary with staffing needs.[3] As discussed in more detail in Chapter Seven, finding military officers with the appropriate advanced academic degrees is more difficult in certain academic disciplines than in others. In particular, given that humanities disciplines are not as aligned as other fields with Air Force career fields, finding military officers with degrees in these disciplines can be challenging. Additionally, some respondents indicated that the mix should be based on departmental preferences in terms of what works best in that department. As one respondent stated,

> I don't know if I can come up with an ideal ratio overall. You have to go at the disaggregate level. What I have now [in my depart-

---

[2] We provide greater detail on the qualitative findings regarding the different roles of military and civilian faculty in later chapters.

[3] USAFA academic departments are as follows: The Basic Sciences Division includes the Departments of Biology, Chemistry, Computer Science, Mathematical Sciences, and Physics; the Engineering Division includes the Departments of Aeronautics, Astronautics, Civil and Environmental Engineering, Electrical and Computer Engineering, and Engineering Mechanics; the Social Sciences Division includes the Departments of Behavioral Sciences and Leadership, Economics and Geosciences, Law, Management, and Political Science; and the Humanities Division includes the Departments of English and Fine Arts, Foreign Languages, History, Military Strategic Studies, and Philosophy. Under the Interdisciplinary Majors designation are the Departments of Meteorology and Operations Research, as well as the Academy's research centers and institutes and the Academy Scholars Program.

ment] feels about right. Other departments have different views about what feels right.

When asked what criteria were used to determine the ideal mix, we again heard similar answers across respondents. Specifically, USAFA senior leaders cited the important differences in the roles of military and civilian faculty in helping the Academy achieve its mission. Specifically, civilian faculty members play a key role in providing academic expertise and helping to maintain USAFA's high academic standards. Therefore, USAFA senior leaders argued, having some civilian faculty members is critical. However, the bottom line for all respondents was that USAFA is a military institution and therefore must have a majority-military faculty. In other words, "warriors best produce warriors."[4]

According to one respondent, "It comes down to maintaining the essential military character of the school; military faculty are essential for that." Similarly, another respondent argued that "the great law schools produce lawyers, and the idea that they should bring on large numbers of non-lawyers to do that would be distinctly odd." Consistent with this, a few respondents also cited the importance of having a majority-military faculty in order to maintain the governance and authority roles occupied by military officers. They expressed concern that changes in governance roles could similarly affect the military culture of USAFA.

Finally, a small number of respondents also cited the importance of maintaining USAFA's ability to have a "second graduating class" among the rotating officers who obtain degrees and teach at USAFA. This was discussed primarily in reference to the more junior rotating officers. Specifically, USAFA leadership argued that a teaching tour provides an important developmental experience for officers by giving them a chance to develop more expertise and depth in that academic discipline. This experience can then benefit the broader Air Force when these officers return to their career fields. As one senior leader stated,

---

[4] Brig Gen Dana Born, "Dean's Response to the Larson Report on the Faculty System at the Air Force Academy," December 3, 2004, p. 4.

"We graduate two graduating classes. For every civilian we bring on board, that is one less developmental opportunity for a military officer."

Summary

Although USAFA senior leaders valued the roles and contributions of both military and civilian faculty, they believed that USAFA faculty must remain majority-military, with an ideal mix of roughly 75 percent military and 25 percent civilians. This was consistent across those we interviewed. In considering the question of the ideal mix, USAFA senior leaders cited the importance of different faculty roles but viewed the military nature of the institution as the most important factor. Several respondents also referenced USAFA's role in producing a "second graduating class" of officers who are sponsored for degrees and then come to teach at USAFA. However, our interviewees also identified several challenges to obtaining this ideal mix, which are discussed in more detail in Chapter Seven.

These perspectives from USAFA leaders may not be surprising given their military background. The findings are also consistent with past arguments made by Air Force leaders (see Appendix A for a more detailed discussion on historical perspectives). During our study, we also elicited the opinions of the civilian faculty at USAFA and examined more-objective evidence regarding faculty quality.

CHAPTER FOUR

Cadets' Officership Development

Given USAFA's primary mission to produce "officers of character," the first factor we examined was cadets' officership development, which we define as the extent to which cadets are socialized into the Air Force culture and the role of being an officer. USAFA senior leaders stressed the importance of officership development as a key criterion in how they thought about the ideal faculty mix, and we assessed the role of faculty in cadets' officership development through those interviews, as well as focus groups with current faculty members, and a survey of cadets.

Interview and Focus Group Findings

As a follow-up to our interviews with USAFA senior leaders, we conducted a set of interviews with ten USAFA faculty in key leadership positions under the Dean of Faculty and held focus groups with current USAFA faculty members.[1] One of the key topic areas for these interviews and focus groups was whether military and civilian faculty members play different roles in helping USAFA achieve its mission and how those roles differ. Not surprisingly, both the senior leaders and the military and civilian faculty members identified military officers as playing a key role in cadets' officership development. Specifically, they described military faculty members as providing

[1] Details about the sample, methodology, and qualitative analysis for our interviews with USAFA senior leaders and focus groups with faculty members can be found in Appendix B.

- military role modeling
- operational experience
- career advice.

Military Role Modeling

Both active-duty military faculty and prior-service civilian faculty mentioned that military faculty acted as role models for cadets as they enter the military profession. According to one faculty member,

> I think there is nothing quite like having a captain with six or seven years of Air Force experience, one or two tours in a laboratory, who can meet with cadets and say, "We're going to learn aeronautical engineering, how planes fly, but I'll also share with you how excited you [should] be about becoming an Air Force officer in a few years, and how you can use what you learn in my class to be better in undergrad pilot training, or in a maintenance squadron, or whatever." So, they are role models and also sources of inspiration for the cadets. Cadets will hopefully look at this captain and say, "In ten years, I want to be like you."

Both senior leaders and faculty members also noted that the junior and senior rotating faculty bring different but complementary characteristics that are beneficial in a military role model. For example, respondents described junior rotating faculty as bringing "energy" and "inspiration" to the classroom and serving as role models to whom cadets could easily relate. Said one faculty member,

> The young people really give a current sense of what's going on now and a role model that the cadets can more directly relate to, and it's who they will be soon. With more senior folks, they maybe provide some more wisdom, big-picture-wise. . . . But in both cases, they provide a role model for the cadets.

Operational Experience

USAFA senior leaders and faculty members also cited the value of the operational experience that military faculty can impart to cadets. For example, one respondent stated, "The military perspective is usually one that includes an understanding of operations and so how to apply the knowledge and skills to Air Force situations." In particular, faculty spoke about how having military experience is important in terms of adding military context to coursework. In the words of one military faculty member, for example,

> Whether it's history, whether it's military strategy, whether it's physics, you can bring that to a military context and give it a relative application: This is why this will be important to you as an officer. This is the value in this learning, and here's how it fits into the whole. I think that's absolutely critical.

Faculty members also spoke specifically about the value of faculty members who have deployed. Finally, faculty members described prior-service faculty members as being able to fulfill this role as well because they are familiar with how the academic discipline is used in the military and what issues cadets are going to encounter as officers.

Career Advice

Related to the operational experience that military faculty are able to bring into the classroom, senior leaders and faculty members also identified the important role that military faculty play in providing career advice to cadets. Noting differences among faculty, one civilian faculty member said, "I can't tell war stories, advice about career fields. So, sure, there is a division of labor."

In summary, USAFA senior leaders and both civilian and military faculty members identified active-duty military faculty as serving a key role in cadets' officership development at USAFA. Specifically, they identified military faculty as being important in serving as role models, bringing real operational experience to the classroom, and providing career advice.

Cadet Survey Findings

To further examine officership development, we conducted a survey of cadets that included questions on how they perceive their interactions with different faculty types (i.e., civilian faculty, civilian faculty with prior service experience, and active-duty military faculty) and the commandant staff responsible for military training (i.e., air officers commanding [AOCs] and academy military trainers [AMTs]) influencing key aspects of their officer development.

A total of 1,642 cadets completed the survey, an initial response rate of 36 percent. We eliminated problematic surveys (i.e., large percentage of unanswered questions, completion time of less than seven minutes, incorrect response to a screening question),[2] which reduced the sample size to 859 participants, for a final response rate of 19 percent. See Appendix C for additional details on the survey methodology and participants.

Survey Content

The survey focused on the extent to which cadets perceived interactions with the following four USAFA groups as influencing key aspects of their development:

1. academic civilian faculty
2. academic civilian faculty with prior service experience
3. academic active-duty military faculty
4. commandant staff (i.e., AOCs and AMTs).

Given the distinction often made between civilians with prior service experience and civilians with no prior service experience, we thought it was important to see if cadets perceived these civilian groups as having different degrees of influence on various aspects of their development. We also included members of the commandant staff (AOCs and AMTs), who are active-duty personnel in charge of military training, as a comparison for active-duty military faculty.[3]

In exploring how USAFA cadets perceived the influence of these different groups on their learning and development, our survey focused

---

2 One item was purposely designed to verify cadet engagement with the survey and detect possible random responses by directing respondents to select a specific response.

3 To focus only on academic faculty, the survey explicitly directed that athletic department faculty should not be included in any of these groups.

primarily on the aspects of cadet learning and development that are specifically stressed in USAFA guidance. USAFA Pamphlet 36-3527, *The Officer Development System: Developing Leaders of Character*, describes the purpose and structure of the Officer Development System, which serves as the overarching doctrinal framework for the systematic development of USAFA cadets. It also addresses the many aspects of cadet learning and development included in the system.[4]

In terms of officer development, we assessed the impact of these groups on the following two outcomes: learning Air Force core values and leadership development.

We also examined potential differences in the following key roles related to officer development that were identified in our qualitative findings: the ability to connect classroom material with the operational Air Force and the ability to provide career advice.

To avoid the influence of any wording bias in a single survey item, we assessed each of these constructs with multiple items. For each item, we asked cadets to rate the extent to which their interactions with each of the four groups contributed to their learning or development using a five-point response scale (1 = "to no extent"; 5 = "to a great extent"). We then averaged the item responses to create a single scale score representing the influence of each of the four groups on each construct.

Survey Results

In the following sections, we present results from the cadet survey. As described in Appendix C, we weighted the responses by cadet class year and academic major to ensure that they represented the cadet population as a whole. Where relevant, we also present results for the class of 2011 only, given that this group had the most exposure to all faculty groups at the time of our study. Cadets in their earlier years generally have a high load of introductory core classes taught by junior rotating military faculty. In contrast, senior USAFA cadets are generally completing their upper-level academic major classes, typically taught by civilian instructors or non-rotational military faculty members with

---

4 See HQ United States Air Force Academy Pamphlet 36-3527, *The Officer Development System: Developing Leaders of Character*, August 11, 2008.

higher advanced degrees. Thus, cadets in the senior class at the time of the survey, the class of 2011, might have had different perceptions regarding the influence of different USAFA academic faculty groups.

Air Force Core Values

According to USAFA Pamphlet 36-3257, Air Force core values are one component of the foundation of character-based officership and serve as the moral code guiding officers in fulfilling their commitment.[5] The Air Force's core values are characterized by the following three mantras: Integrity First, Service Before Self, and Excellence in All We Do. We developed the following three survey items to examine the influence of each USAFA group on cadets' development of the Air Force's core values.

> To what extent have your interactions with the following groups contributed to your
>
> 1. learning how to act in accordance with the Air Force core value of Integrity First?
> 2. learning how to act in accordance with the Air Force core value of Service Before Self?
> 3. learning how to act in accordance with the Air Force core value of Excellence in All We Do?[6]

Figure 4.1 shows mean scores for the extent to which interactions with each group influenced cadet learning of Air Force core values. As the figure shows, cadets reported that all the groups had some influence on their development of Air Force core values. However, as would be expected given the characterization of active-duty military faculty

---

5 HQ United States Air Force Academy Pamphlet 36-3257, 2008.

6 To support the averaging of these items into a single, unified scale for each group (resulting in a total of four scales), we conducted an exploratory factor analysis, which is a statistical procedure designed to assess the extent to which the items are measuring a single theme. We also examined the extent to which each scale demonstrated acceptable reliability or internal consistency by calculating Cronbach's alpha for each scale. Generally, a value greater than 0.70 is considered to indicate acceptable reliability (Nunnally and Bernstein, 1994). Each of the four scales (separate scale for each group) demonstrated acceptable reliability or internal consistency (α ranged from 0.84 to 0.87 across the scales).

Figure 4.1
Influence on Learning of Air Force Core Values

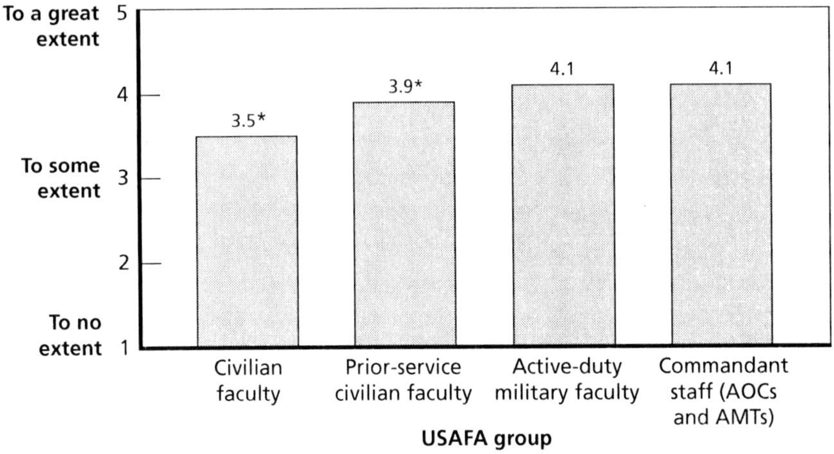

NOTE: N = 845. Results represent weighted responses. All pairwise tests were conducted; * indicates a mean score that has a statistically significant difference from all other groups, $p \leq 0.05$.
RAND *MG1237-4.1*

as military role models, cadets reported their interactions with active-duty military faculty and commandant staff members (AOCs and AMTs) as having the greatest influence on their learning to act in accordance with Air Force core values. Additionally, although there was a statistically significant difference, cadets rated prior-service civilian faculty as having a fairly comparable influence as the two military groups. Cadets rated civilian faculty with no prior service experience as having the least amount of influence on cadet learning of Air Force core values. We found a similar pattern of results when we examined the class of 2011 only.

Leadership Development

As part of officer development, USAFA outlines four levels of leadership competencies that all cadets are expected to develop during their four years at the Academy. The PITO model, for Personal, Interpersonal, Team, and Organizational, defines the competencies for each year of the cadet's leadership development process. In describing this model, USAFA Pamphlet 36-3257 states that cadets must "internalize foundational, personal elements before they can successfully execute interpersonal leadership skills."[7] Only after mastering these basic competencies can a cadet move on to lead a team or an organization. Using the PITO model, we developed multiple survey items designed to separately measure the broader PITO leadership constructs. Cadets were asked to answer only the items associated with their class year, however. Thus, for example, first-year cadets were not asked questions about their team or organizational leadership development.

We developed four to five items to measure each leadership development level. For all items, cadets were asked, "To what extent have your interactions with the following groups contributed to [various aspects of your officer development]?" An example of an item for *personal leadership* development is "learning how to set an example of professionalism to others." An example for *interpersonal leadership* development is "learning how to communicate effectively with others." An example for *team leadership* development is "learning how to get team members to work together." An example for *organizational leadership* development is "learning how to motivate all members of an organization to perform to the best of their ability."[8]

The general pattern of results was consistent across the leadership constructs in terms of the influence of each group. Figure 4.2 provides an example of the pattern using the results from the interpersonal leadership development scale. As the figure shows, although all pairwise comparisons were statistically significant ($p \leq 0.05$),[9] overall, there were only minimal differences in how cadets rated the four groups. In terms of academic faculty, cadets rated active-duty military faculty as having a slightly greater influence than both civilian faculty groups. This is again consistent with the assertion that military faculty play a

---

7 See HQ United States Air Force Academy Pamphlet 36-3257, 2008, p. 10.

8 See Appendix C for a full list of the survey items. We performed an exploratory factor analysis to support our averaging of items into a single, unified scale for each leadership construct and group. Each of the leadership construct scales demonstrated acceptable reliability (α ranged from 0.83 to 0.98 across the scales).

9 Differences in mean scores across groups were statistically significant ($p \leq 0.05$) for all leadership constructs, except for the difference between active-duty military faculty and commandant staff members for the development of organizational leadership.

Figure 4.2
Influence on Cadets' Interpersonal Leadership Development

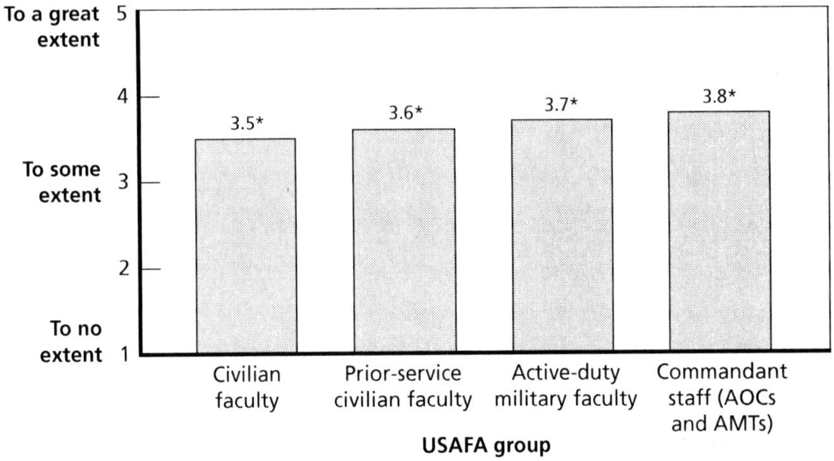

NOTE: $N = 844$. Results represent weighted responses. All pairwise tests were conducted; * indicates a mean score that has a statistically significant difference from all other groups, $p \leq 0.05$.
RAND *MG1237-4.2*

critical role in cadets' officership development. However, overall, cadets reported their interactions with commandant staff members (AOCs and AMTs) as having the greatest influence on their leadership development. We found a similar pattern of results when we examined the class of 2011 only.

Because the basic tenets of each PITO model level are generally aligned with the actual positions cadets assume in their cadet squadrons, which are guided by AOCs and AMTs, it makes sense that cadets would perceive commandant staff members as having the greatest influence on their learning the PITO model competencies. For example, AOCs and AMTs generally counsel cadets in their chain of command on how well they are operating in these areas.

Ability to Connect the Classroom to the Air Force

As described earlier, our qualitative findings indicated that military faculty members play a unique role in their ability to connect classroom material to actual Air Force situations and cadets' potential future careers. Therefore, we developed the following two items to assess whether cadets perceived this different role among faculty members. We did not ask cadets to rate commandant staff members, however, since they provide military training and not academic instruction.

> To what extent do the following groups
> 1. use relevant Air Force examples to explain key concepts in class?
> 2. have knowledge of recent Air Force situations that relate to course content?[10]

Figure 4.3 shows the mean scores for the extent to which different faculty groups were able to connect classroom material to the Air Force. As the figure shows, cadets reported active-duty military faculty as best able to provide relevant Air Force examples to explain

Figure 4.3
Ability to Connect Classroom Content to the Air Force

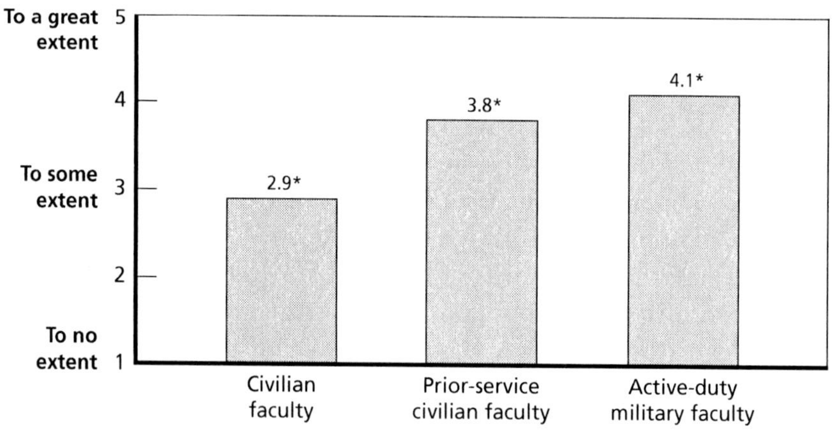

NOTE: $N = 844$. Results represent weighted responses. All pairwise tests were conducted; * indicates a mean score that has a statistically significant difference from all other groups, $p \leq 0.05$.
RAND *MG1237-4.3*

---

[10] We performed an exploratory factor analysis to support our averaging of items into a single, unified scale for each faculty group. The scales also demonstrated acceptable reliability (α ranged from 0.77 to 0.80 across scales).

key concepts and demonstrate knowledge of recent Air Force situations during classroom instruction. This was followed by prior-service civilian faculty and civilian faculty with no prior service. Differences in mean scores across all three faculty groups were statistically significant ($p \leq 0.05$). These results are not surprising given that active-duty military faculty have operational experience that civilian faculty do not and that is more recent than the experiences of prior-service civilian faculty. We found a similar pattern of results when we examined the class of 2011 only.

Career Advice

Our qualitative findings also indicated that military faculty members play an important role in providing career advice to cadets. Therefore, we developed the following four items to assess cadet perceptions of the ability of each group to provide career advice:

> To what extent have your interactions with the following groups contributed to your
>
> 1. knowledge of different career options within the Air Force?
> 2. knowledge of the types of assignments you would receive with different Air Force Specialty Codes (AFSCs)?
> 3. knowledge of the kinds of training you would experience with different Air Force Specialty Codes (AFSCs)?
> 4. intended (or awarded) choice of Air Force Specialty Code (AFSC)?[11]

Figure 4.4 shows the mean scores for the extent to which different USAFA groups are best able to provide Air Force career advice. As the figure shows, cadets rated active-duty military faculty and commandant staff members (AOCs and AMTs) as best able to provide Air Force career advice. This is not surprising given that both of these groups consist of active-duty military personnel from various career fields who are familiar with various Air Force assignments and organi-

[11] We performed an exploratory factory analysis to support our averaging of these items into a single unified scale for each faculty group. The scales also demonstrated acceptable reliability (α ranged from 0.85 to 0.88 across scales).

Figure 4.4
Ability to Provide Career Advice

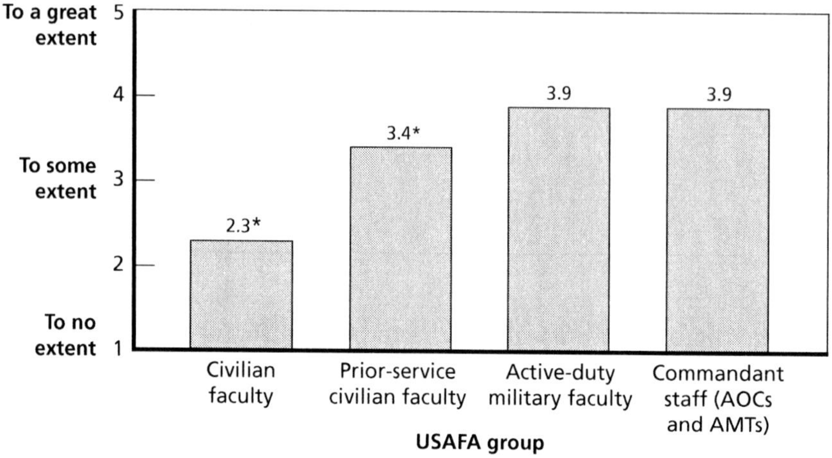

NOTE: $N = 841$. Results represent weighted responses. All pairwise tests were conducted; * indicates a mean score that has a statistically significant difference from all other groups, $p \leq 0.05$.
RAND *MG1237-4.4*

zational duty locations. They can also advise cadets on issues that are relevant to the decisions that cadets will have to make as they progress in their own intended career paths. Cadets also rated prior-service civilian faculty members as able to provide career advice, although to a significantly lesser extent than active-duty military personnel and commandant staff ($p \leq 0.05$). Prior-service civilian faculty also possess some knowledge of different military career and assignment options, but their knowledge is likely less current compared with that of individuals on active duty. Finally, as would be expected, cadets rated civilian faculty with no prior service experience as significantly less able to provide career advice compared with all other groups ($p \leq 0.05$). We found a similar pattern of results when we examined the class of 2011 only.

Survey Limitations

Although the differences were often small, as would be expected, active-duty military faculty and commandant staff were consistently rated as having a greater impact on aspects of cadets' officership development as measured by the cadet survey. It is important to note, however, that the survey had several limitations. First, the overall response rate across cadets was relatively low, at 19 percent. This suggests that some caution should be used in generalizing the findings to the broader cadet population. Second, there are many potential differences in the impact of civilian and military faculty on cadets that cannot be measured on a survey. Thus, we were not able to assess how some of the different roles and contributions of these faculty types ultimately affect cadets. In addition, the survey results represent perceptions only; actual impact on cadet development may differ from what cadets are able to perceive. Furthermore, although we thought it important to make a distinction between civilian faculty with no prior service experience and those with prior service experience, cadets may not always be aware of this status for each faculty member. Additionally, the survey was administered to current cadets. A survey of officers who graduated from USAFA a few years earlier, such as first lieutenants, may have provided different perspectives on the role of these faculty types. Finally, it is important to note that the majority of faculty members are active-duty military personnel. Therefore, some of the results reported here may simply reflect the greater amount of time spent with military faculty than with civilian faculty members.

Summary

Although we were not able to directly measure the impact that different faculty types have on cadets' officership development, both our qualitative findings and survey of cadets provide important insight into this factor. Specifically, USAFA senior leaders and faculty in our focus groups identified military faculty as playing a key role in cadets' officership development by serving as role models, relating their operational experiences in the classroom, and providing career advice. Findings from the survey of cadets further support this distinction in faculty roles. Although the differences were often small, cadets rated active-duty military faculty as having the greatest influence on aspects of officer development compared with civilian and prior-service civilian faculty. The results also indicate that civilians with prior service experience fulfill somewhat in-between roles. Given that these faculty members have prior military experience, cadets rated them as having a greater impact on aspects of officer development compared with civilians with no prior military experience. However, their impact was still lower than that of active-duty military faculty.

Additionally, the data show that commandant staff members (AOCs and AMTs) were perceived as having greater or equal influence on aspects of cadets' officer development compared with active-duty academic faculty members. The large role that commandant staff members play in cadets' officership development also raises the question of whether it is necessary for all academic faculty members to provide officership development in the same way. Unlike academic development, which requires all faculty members to provide high-quality instruction to cadets, it is not as clear whether the development of officers requires similar role modeling by all faculty members in addition to the structured role modeling and military training provided by commandant staff members (AOCs and AMTs). For example, officers who have commissioned through the Reserve Officer Training Corps (ROTC) and Officer Training School (OTS) would not have received instruction from military academic faculty but instead would have attended civilian institutions while also being provided additional military training. Certainly, organizational psychology theory suggests that the people within an organization influence the organizational culture and the climate that develops.[12] Therefore, a greater military presence among faculty and staff will likely translate to a more visible military culture in the institution. However, the extent to which this is critical to develop officers remains unclear and represents a limitation of the study.

---

[12] See Cheri Ostroff, Angelo J. Kinicki, and Melinda M. Tamkins, "Organizational Culture and Climate," *Handbook of Psychology*, Vol. 12: *Industrial and Organizational Psychology*, Hoboken, N.J.: Wiley, 2003.

CHAPTER FIVE

Cadets' Academic Development

Although USAFA is responsible for commissioning officers into the Air Force, it also provides a high-quality four-year college education. Therefore, we identified academics and the extent to which cadets are provided a rigorous and intellectually challenging education as critical factors in our analysis. We assessed the role of faculty in cadets' academic development through four key sources of information: (1) data provided by USAFA on the academic qualifications of its faculty members, (2) findings from our USAFA senior leader interviews and faculty focus groups, (3) results from our survey of cadets, and (4) a quantitative analysis of potential differences in the teaching effectiveness of military and civilian faculty members.

Academic Background Characteristics

Based on data provided by USAFA,[1] there are several key differences in the academic-related background characteristics of military and civilian faculty. First, there is a considerable difference in teaching experience given that academia is not the main career path for military personnel. Civilian faculty members had a self-reported average of 13.6 years of experience teaching at USAFA and other academic institutions, while military faculty members had an average of only

[1] The information provided by USAFA was based on self-reported data on all faculty teaching at the Academy at the time of our research. The data were subsequently reviewed by academic department representatives and the Vice Dean of Faculty to verify accuracy.

3.1 years of teaching experience. Further, given the rotational nature of the military faculty, most had never taught before coming to USAFA.

In addition to teaching experience, as Table 5.1 shows, the vast majority of civilian faculty members have doctoral degrees, compared with only around a third of military faculty members.

Table 5.1
Distribution of Degrees Among Faculty

Degree	% of Military Faculty (*n* = 378)	% of Civilian Faculty (*n* = 153)
Master's[a]	62	10
Doctorate	33	86
Juris doctor	5	2
Other	—	1

NOTE: Percentages do not include temporary faculty, only faculty in authorized billets.

[a] Includes faculty members who have a master's degree and may have completed some additional coursework to receive a higher degree but have not yet completed the higher degree.

Finally, as Table 5.2 shows, because civilian faculty generally spend a greater amount of time teaching at USAFA compared with military faculty who serve rotating tours, civilian faculty also tend to hold much higher academic ranks across departments. Current governing rules do not permit civilian faculty to hold departmental leadership positions, however.[2] In contrast, junior rotating military faculty compose almost all of the lower-level instructor positions.

Thus, based on these data, civilian faculty members are more likely to be seasoned instructors and bring a greater depth of expertise to the classroom due to their doctoral training. These characteristics are also particularly critical in meeting academic accreditation standards.

[2] In some cases, civilian faculty members have served as interim department chairs.

Table 5.2
Distribution of Academic Rank Among Faculty

Faculty Position	% of Military Faculty (*n* = 378)	% of Civilian Faculty (*n* = 153)
Instructor	43	<1
Assistant professor	47	26
Associate professor	4	23
Professor	6	43
Visiting professor	—	7

NOTE: Percentages do not include temporary faculty, only faculty in authorized billets.

Interview and Focus Group Findings

As described earlier, one of the key topic areas we examined as part of our interviews with USAFA senior leaders and our focus groups with current faculty members was whether military and civilian faculty play different roles in helping USAFA achieve its mission and how those roles differ.[3] Consistent with these groups' differences in background characteristics, USAFA senior leaders and faculty members in our focus groups identified civilians as playing a key academic role at USAFA. Specifically, they described civilian faculty members as providing

- continuity and stability
- academic rigor and teaching expertise
- connections with broader academia and the research community
- diverse perspectives.

Continuity and Stability

Both USAFA senior leaders and faculty members identified one of the key assets of civilian faculty as providing continuity and stability to the academic programs at USAFA. Except for a small group of permanent

[3] Refer to Appendix B for more details on participants and methodology.

professors and senior military faculty, the large majority of military faculty members serve rotating tours at USAFA that generally last only three to four years. In contrast, civilian faculty members have a much longer tenure at the Academy. Therefore, they are the faculty members who are most familiar with the curriculum and academic programs, and they act as the "keepers of the continuity of educational programs."

Civilian faculty members, in turn, were concerned about the high turnover among military faculty. In our focus groups, they described the difficulties of bringing in junior military instructors with no teaching experience for short tours: "The challenge is that we have people with a one-year master's, no teaching experience, and they rotate in and out," said one civilian faculty member. As discussed previously, this concern is consistent with past criticisms of the service academies and is one of the reasons that Congress pushed for the incorporation of civilian faculty members.

Academic Rigor and Teaching Expertise

Both USAFA senior leaders and current faculty also described civilians as being the subject-matter experts in their departments and providing "academic rigor." According to one respondent, civilians "provide a depth of academic expertise that is generally not available with our rotating military faculty; [the latter] tend to have master's degrees, whereas the vast majority of civilians have doctorates." Similarly, a civilian faculty member described one of the roles of civilians as maintaining high academic standards: "I really see, especially as academics, civilians, our charge is, in part, to make sure that high academic standards stay really paramount."

Related to civilian faculty members' academic expertise, both USAFA senior leaders and faculty also identified civilians as providing much of the teaching expertise at USAFA and playing a key role in curriculum development and mentoring of more junior faculty. As discussed earlier, on average, civilian faculty have considerably more teaching experience than the rotating military faculty members. In fact, most military faculty members have no teaching experience prior to coming to USAFA. Thus, civilians were identified as being responsible for curriculum development and mentoring junior faculty in teaching methods. For example, one civilian faculty member described his role as follows:

> As a regular civilian guy in our department, [I can say that] we're curricular chiefs. I see my main role as making sure that the curriculum looks OK, the right people are teaching it, to maintain some level of quality in that curriculum.

Consistent with this perception, an academic department head stated, "In my department, my civilians are what I call curriculum chiefs: They're the disciplinary subject-matter experts, the experts in that area, and they own the curriculum."

Connections with Broader Academia and the Research Community

USAFA senior leaders and faculty also identified civilians as providing an important connection to broader academia and the research community. Many civilians had worked at other academic institutions and belong to professional academic societies. Furthermore, civilian faculty members at USAFA are expected to engage in research and publishing, which are considered during promotion evaluations. In contrast, rotating military faculty do not remain at USAFA for a long enough period to engage in long-term research efforts.

Diverse Perspectives

Finally, respondents described civilian faculty as providing a valuable outside perspective. For example, in discussing the value of civilians at USAFA, one faculty member commented, "It's a great mix. It's great for [the cadets] to see a different perspective, from a diversity point of view." Similarly, a military faculty member stated,

> Is it important for cadets to get a different view than straight military? I think them seeing someone else—and they'll work with civilians—helps them to see more of the outside world. In the military, you can get a kind of tunnel vision; your whole life is in the military. [It] serves to broaden horizons, whether prior or non-prior service.

In summary, USAFA senior leaders and both civilian and military faculty members identified civilians as serving a key academic role at USAFA, in contrast to military officers, whom they identified as playing a more prominent role in officership development. Specifically, they identified civilian faculty as being important to providing continuity and stability in the academic programs, teaching expertise and academic rigor, and connections to broader academia and the research community, as well as bringing the potential for a different perspective from that of military faculty members.

Cadet Survey Findings

To further examine cadets' academic development, we included questions on the cadet survey that focused on the extent to which cadets perceived an influence on key aspects of their academic development as a result of interactions with different faculty types (civilian faculty, civilian faculty with prior service experience, and active-duty military faculty) and commandant staff responsible for military training (AOCs and AMTs). Specifically, we assessed the impact of these groups on cadets' intellectual skill development and the extent to which cadets perceived differences in the depth of knowledge that faculty brought to the classroom, such as was identified in our interviews and focus groups.

To avoid the influence of any wording bias in a single item, we assessed each topic area or construct with multiple items. For each item, we asked cadets to rate the extent to which their interactions with each faculty group contributed to their learning or development using a five-point response scale (1 = "to no extent"; 5 = "to a great extent"). We then averaged the item responses for each topic area or construct to create a single scale score representing the influence of the four groups on each construct.

We again weighted the responses by cadet class year and academic major to ensure that they represented the cadet population as a whole. Where relevant, we also present results for the class of 2011 only, since this class had the most exposure to all faculty groups.

Intellectual Skill Development

Intellectual skill development in several specific areas is one of USAFA's key outcomes for officers upon graduation.[4] Given the responsibility of faculty members to oversee academics at USAFA, we examined the extent to which cadets perceived an influence from these different groups on their intellectual skill development. Using the specific intellectual skills outlined by USAFA as part of its outcomes, we developed the following five items:

> To what extent have your interactions with the following groups contributed to your
>
> 1. learning the skills to effectively analyze quantitative problems?
> 2. learning the skills to effectively use different sources of information to solve a problem?
> 3. learning the skills to communicate effectively with others?
> 4. learning the skills to critically analyze a problem?
> 5. learning the skills to make effective decisions?[5]

Figure 5.1 shows mean scores for the extent to which different groups influenced cadets' intellectual development. As would be expected for the development of intellectual skills, all three types of academic faculty had statistically significant higher mean scores than commandant staff members (AOCs and AMTs) who focus on military training ($p \leq 0.05$).[6] Although active-duty military faculty were rated as having a statistically significant greater influence compared with the two civilian faculty groups, the actual difference is very minor and likely not practically significant.

---

[4] U.S. Air Force Academy, 2009.

[5] We performed an exploratory factor analysis to support the averaging of these items into a single, unified scale for each faculty group. The scales also demonstrated acceptable reliability (α ranged from 0.89 to 0.91 across scales).

[6] If we examined these items individually, commandant staff members were rated as having an influence similar to that of the other USAFA groups on two of the skill development items: "the ability to communicate effectively with others" and "the ability to make effective decisions." This is not surprising, since these skills are also expected to develop as part of the PITO leadership model.

Figure 5.1
Influence on Intellectual Skill Development

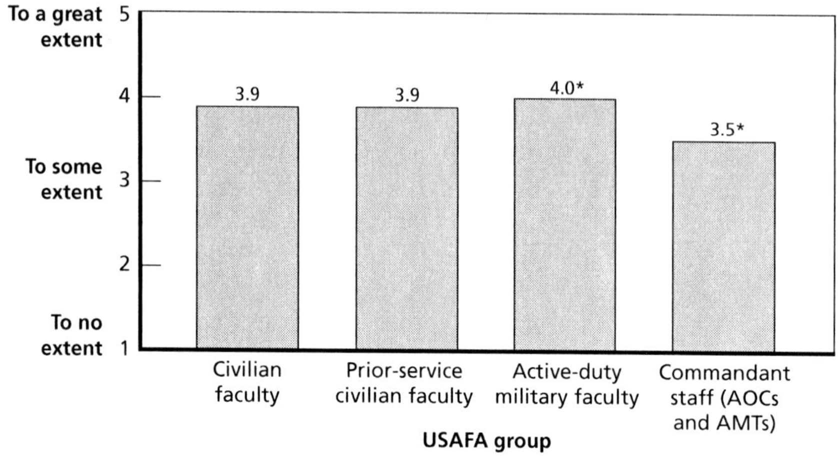

NOTE: $N = 840$. Results represent weighted responses. All pairwise tests were conducted; * indicates a mean score that has a statistically significant difference from all other groups, $p \leq 0.05$.
RAND *MG1237-5.1*

When examining the responses of the class of 2011 alone, we found no statistically significant difference in the mean scores across all three of the academic faculty groups, indicating that, on average, cadets in the class of 2011 perceived all faculty members as having an equal influence on their intellectual skill development.

Faculty Academic Depth of Knowledge

To further examine the academic role of civilian faculty—specifically, their role in providing academic expertise and insight into recent research in their field—we assessed the extent to which cadets perceived differences in faculty members' academic depth of knowledge with the following three items:

During class time, to what extent do the follow groups

1. discuss their knowledge of recent research related to the class material?

2. discuss how the material being taught in class is applicable to situations beyond the military context?
3. discuss the latest developments in the academic subject being taught in class?[7]

Figure 5.2 shows mean scores for the extent to which cadets perceived differences in faculty academic depth of knowledge. As the figure shows, although both civilian faculty groups were rated as having a statistically significant greater influence than active-duty military faculty, the actual difference was very minor and likely not practically significant. Results based on the responses from the class of 2011 show a similar overall pattern, except that this group rated civilian faculty with no prior service experience as having a slightly greater academic depth of knowledge than prior-service civilian faculty.

Figure 5.2
Perceived Faculty Academic Depth of Knowledge

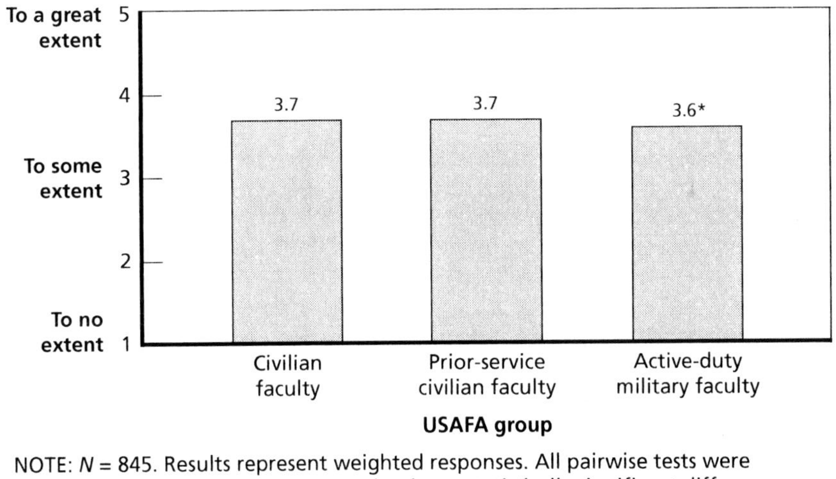

NOTE: *N* = 845. Results represent weighted responses. All pairwise tests were conducted; * indicates a mean score that has a statistically significant difference from all other groups, $p \leq 0.05$.
RAND *MG1237-5.2*

[7] We performed an exploratory factor analysis to support the averaging of these items into a single, unified scale for each faculty group. The scales also demonstrated acceptable reliability (α ranged from 0.76 to 0.81 across scales).

Importance of Faculty Characteristics

Finally, the survey included one item that asked cadets to rate the importance of various faculty characteristics when taking a course at USAFA. Rather than using a five-point response scale, this survey item presented cadets with five different faculty characteristics that they were asked to rank in order of importance, with 1 indicating the most important characteristic and 5 indicating the least important characteristic.

As Table 5.3 shows, "how knowledgeable an instructor is of the given course topic" took priority for cadets, with the largest percentage (44 percent) rating this characteristic as the most important. Fewer cadets rated "the extent to which the instructor discusses applications

Table 5.3
Importance of Academic Faculty Characteristics

	Cadet Rating (%)				
Faculty Characteristic	**Most Important**	**2nd Most Important**	**3rd Most Important**	**4th Most Important**	**Least Important**
How knowledgeable the instructor is of the course topic	44	21	15	11	9
The extent to which the instructor teaches the material in a way that will be useful to your future military career	20	26	22	20	12
The teaching experience of the instructor	17	17	15	16	34
The extent to which the instructor discusses applications of course material beyond the military	9	22	25	23	19
The extent to which the instructor is a good military role model	9	13	24	29	25

NOTE: *N* = 845. Percentages may not sum to 100 percent due to rounding.

of course material beyond the military" and "the extent to which the instructor is a good military role model" as most important (9 percent).

Overall, the results from the cadet survey indicate only very minimal differences in the influence of various USAFA groups on cadets' academic development, with no significant differences when examining the class of 2011 only. As discussed in Chapter Four, however, these findings represent perceptions, and the extent to which there is a practical impact on cadet academic development is unclear. Furthermore, the same limitations with regard to the cadet survey described in Chapter Four apply to these findings. In particular, some of the results reported here may simply reflect the greater amount of time cadets spend with military faculty members due to their greater representation on the faculty.

Relative Teaching Effectiveness

To provide a more objective examination of potential differences in faculty influence on cadets' academic development, we also statistically examined whether faculty type (i.e., civilian faculty, civilian faculty with prior service experience, and active-duty military faculty) has an influence on actual student learning at USAFA using a small sample of data on faculty who taught introductory courses between 1997 and 2007. Specifically, we used a statistical method known as a "value-added approach" that is designed to examine the impact of instructor type on student performance in an introductory course and in a follow-on course, which is "arguably a more persistent measure of student learning."[8]

Study Setting

USAFA provides a unique setting for examining teaching effectiveness in that all students are required to complete a set of core courses during their first two years. Because all USAFA students must complete these courses, enrollment in a core course offering typically ranges from

[8] Scott Carrell and James West, "Does Professor Quality Matter? Evidence from Random Assignment of Students to Professors," *Journal of Political Economy*, Vol. 118, No. 3, 2010, p. 411.

400 to 700 students, depending on the size of the entering class and the number of teaching faculty available. To keep the student-to-teacher ratio low, multiple sections of the same course are taught by different faculty members. In many of these core courses, faculty members teaching different sections use an identical syllabus and evaluate students using the same assignments and exams during common testing periods. As a result, these more standardized courses allow for a consistent measure of student learning via student grades across different sections of a given course. Another unique aspect of the course structure at USAFA is that students have no means of choosing their desired instructor for a given course. USAFA uses an algorithm to randomly assign students to sections of a course, thus eliminating the possibility of students self-selecting into or out of given sections based on the faculty member teaching that section.[9]

Finally, while a large variety of courses are taught at USAFA, there is a smaller subset of subject areas in which all students are required to take an introductory core course and a subsequent single follow-on course in the same subject area. In this setup, USAFA randomly assigns each student to an introductory core course section, and, after completing this introductory core course, the student is again randomly placed into a section of the follow-on course. Subject areas employing this configuration include math, chemistry, physics, and history.

These courses exhibit varying degrees of uniformity of instruction and student evaluation across sections, however, with the introductory and follow-on math courses being the most standardized. Faculty members use the same syllabus in instructing their sections and administer the same exams to students during a common testing period, and all faculty members are given a copy of the course exams prior to the start

---

[9] Randomized class assignments appear to work as stated. To examine the effectiveness of the randomized assignment to classes, we regressed student and section averaged pretreatment SAT and academic composite scores on the faculty type indicators for the respective courses. These results are presented in Appendix D. In a few instances, student- and section-level characteristics exhibited statistically significant differences across the three different types of USAFA faculty in the courses examined, but the differences do not appear to be practically significant. In other words, there is no systematic evidence of purposive student sorting or preferential assignments of certain faculty types to more academically qualified or less academically qualified students.

of the semester. The grading of math exams is also standardized. Teams of professors teaching the same course jointly grade all exams, with a single professor grading all student responses to a single exam question. This standardization of grading in the core math courses removes any possibility that different professors have different degrees of influence on exam grades. In this sense, given the standardization in the syllabus, testing, and evaluation across the core math sections, it is more likely that differences in student performance, when controlling for student- and section-level characteristics, will be a result of differences in the instruction employed by a given section's instructor.

Therefore, we focused our analysis primarily on required core math courses to best determine whether military or civilian faculty type has an effect on student achievement. We also modeled student achievement in other required core courses with a similar introductory and follow-on course configuration to provide some generalizability to other subject areas. Of course, the instruction and grading in these courses is less standardized, making the modeled results relatively less accurate than those for the math courses.

Data

Our data consisted of information related to the previously described courses for students who attended USAFA between the fall of 1997 and the spring of 2007.[10] Given the distinction between civilian faculty with prior service experience and faculty with no prior service experience, we chose to examine the teaching effectiveness of these faculty groups separately. Therefore, indicator variables characterizing an individual faculty member as active-duty military, civilian, or civilian with prior service experience functioned as the primary independent

---

[10] Although data exist for USAFA student course scores through 2010, due to changes in course structure in 2007, our analysis used student course scores through academic year 2006–2007 only. While there were no instructor-specific assignments in the Math 141 and Math 142 curriculum until 2007, the math department introduced writing assignments into the curriculum of these courses in the fall 2007 semester. This addition somewhat diminished the degree of standardization between course sections because section instructors graded these writing assignments independent of other section instructors, opening the possibility of inconsistency in grading approaches across sections.

variables of interest in this analysis. Table 5.4 shows the number of active-duty military faculty, civilian faculty, and civilian faculty with prior military service for each semester-year offering of the introduc-

Table 5.4
Introductory Math Faculty Types, by Semester and Year

Semester and Year	Civilian	Prior-Service Civilian	Military	Missing Data	Total
Fall 1997	1	1	7	1	10
Spring 1998	0	0	3	0	3
Fall 1998	2	0	9	0	11
Spring 1999	0	0	4	0	4
Fall 1999	0	0	10	0	10
Spring 2000	0	0	3	0	3
Fall 2000	0	0	11	0	11
Spring 2001	0	1	3	0	4
Fall 2001	0	2	8	0	10
Spring 2002	1	0	2	1	4
Fall 2002	3	1	5	0	9
Spring 2003	1	0	5	0	6
Fall 2003	1	1	6	0	8
Spring 2004	0	0	2	0	2
Fall 2004	1	0	9	0	10
Spring 2005	0	0	2	0	2
Fall 2005	1	0	11	0	12
Spring 2006	0	0	2	0	2
Fall 2006	1	1	11	0	13
Spring 2007	1	0	2	0	3
Total	13	7	115	2	137

tory math course.[11] It is important to note that our overall sample size for civilian faculty members was relatively small, particularly when they are split into the two categories of civilians and civilians with prior service experience. Due to this lower statistical power, our analysis was limited in being able to find significant differences between groups. Additional details regarding the data for the initial and follow-on courses examined are available in Appendix D.

We measured student performance, our dependent variable, as the normalized student grade. For the purposes of computing a given student's overall grade point average, USAFA assigns each student a numeric value respective to their earned alphabetical grade in a course. A student earning an alphabetical grade of A, A–, B+, B, B–, C+, C, D, or F in a course will be given a numerical grade value of 4, 3.7, 3.3, 3, 2.7, 2.3, 2, 1, or 0, respectively. We normalized these equivalent numerical grades to have a mean of zero and a standard deviation of one within each course and semester-year.

Finally, we controlled for student-level characteristics and section-level mean characteristics that could potentially affect student performance in an effort to isolate the independent effect of the variable of interest—the type of faculty associated with each student performance outcome. These variables are listed in Tables 5.5 and 5.6.

In terms of controlling for faculty characteristics beyond the military/civilian distinction, the only additional faculty-level characteristic we included was a dummy variable indicating whether the faculty member was male or female, because this has been shown to have some impact on cadets' performance in math and science classes in previous research.[12]

Results

We used mixed-effects models to examine whether military and civilian faculty members have a different impact on student achievement at

---

[11] Overall, missing data made up only a small percentage of the observations and were dropped from the data included in the analysis.

[12] Scott Carrell, Marianne E. Page, and James E. West, "Sex and Science: How Professor Gender Perpetuates the Gender Gap," *Quarterly Journal of Economics*, August 2010.

Table 5.5
Student-Level Characteristics

Variable	Description
SAT math	SAT math score divided by 100
SAT verbal	SAT verbal score divided by 100
Academic composite score	Academic composite score divided by 100 (includes an applicant's high school class rank, high school grade point average, high school transcript grades, rigor of the high school's curriculum, and the applicant's SAT/ACT scores)
Leadership composite score	Leadership composite score divided by 100 (factors in a USAFA applicant's high school activities, leadership activities, and other activities listed on his or her resume)
Candidate fitness test score	Candidate fitness test score divided by 100 (a physical fitness test of USAFA applicants; consists of a basketball throw, pull-ups, shuttle run, modified sit-ups, push-ups, and a 1-mile run, which all USAFA applicants must complete)
Recruited athlete	Indicates whether the student was a recruited athlete
Prep school	Indicates whether the student attended the USAFA Prep School
Female	Indicates the student's sex
Freshman	Indicates that student was a freshman
Class year	Indicates the student's graduating class

Table 5.6
Section-Level Peer Characteristics

Variable	Description
SAT verbal	Average SAT verbal score
SAT math	Average SAT math score
Academic composite score	Average academic composite score
Section period	Time during the day when the section is held

USAFA.[13] We constructed separate mixed-effects models to explore the value-added of introductory course professors on introductory course student achievement and the value-added of introductory course professors on follow-on course student achievement. Normalized course scores served as measures of student achievement in this context. See Appendix D for more detail on the statistical analyses.

Table 5.7 shows the coefficients for faculty type related to a given introductory math course instructor's value-added in the contemporaneous introductory course and in the mandatory math follow-on course. Each coefficient reported in the table indicates the effect of civilian (or prior-service civilian) faculty on students' performance compared with military faculty. For example, in Table 5.7, students taught by civilian faculty scored lower by –0.05 standard deviations than students taught by military faculty. However, this difference is not statistically significant. Hence, the results indicate that there is no statistically significant relationship between faculty type and student performance in either the introductory math course or the follow-on course after controlling for other variables in the model.

Given the small sample size of civilian faculty, particularly when they are split into the two categories of civilians and civilians with prior service experience, we also reran the above analysis without the distinction between civilian faculty to obtain more statistical power. The results of this analysis also did not show any statistically significant dif-

Table 5.7
Coefficients from the Mixed-Effects Model for an Introductory Math Course Instructor's Value-Added

Variable	Introductory Math Course	Follow-On Math Course
Civilian vs. military	–0.05 (0.062)	0.02 (0.047)
Prior-service civilian vs. military	–0.05 (0.077)	0.03 (0.052)

NOTE: Standard errors are in parentheses.

[13] James West, former professor of economics, USAFA, assisted in the data analysis.

ferences in the teaching effectiveness of civilian faculty compared with active-duty military faculty.

Although the other subject areas with mandatory introductory courses and follow-on courses are not as standardized as the math courses at USAFA, we explored whether faculty type provided significant value-added in these other courses using the same mixed-effects modeling approach. Because student achievement in math courses was more consistently measured, we consider the results relevant to introductory and follow-on math courses foremost and acknowledge that it provides more valid evidence than for other subjects. However, examining math alone may limit the findings. Therefore, we also conducted analyses for non-math core subjects. Results from these analyses are presented in Tables 5.8 and 5.9.

Based on the results shown in Table 5.8, one cannot make any statistically significant conclusions regarding the effect of the different introductory course faculty types on student achievement in the contemporaneous course.

Table 5.8
Coefficients from the Mixed-Effects Model for an Introductory Course Instructor's Value-Added in Contemporaneous Course

Variable	Chemistry	Physics	History
Civilian vs. military	−0.06 (0.045)	0.07 (0.053)	0.06 (0.093)
Prior-service civilian vs. military	0.06 (0.068)	−0.06 (0.057)	0.2 (0.139)

NOTE: Standard errors are in parentheses.

Table 5.9 shows the results for the effect that different types of introductory course professors have on students' performance in a follow-on course. The model of follow-on student performance accounts for the effect of different introductory course faculty types on follow-on course student performance, as well as the effect that different follow-on course faculty types may have on student performance in the follow-on course.

Table 5.9
Coefficients from the Mixed-Effects Model for an Introductory Course Instructor's Value-Added in a Mandatory Follow-On Course

Variable	Chemistry	Physics	History
Civilian vs. military	0.03 (0.027)	NA	−0.03 (0.031)
Prior-service civilian vs. military	0.01 (0.044)	NA	−0.01 (0.074)

NOTE: Standard errors are in parentheses.

The data show that, as with the effect of different introductory math course faculty types on follow-on student achievement in math, differences between initial course faculty types across the other subject areas studied are not statistically significant. The table does not show results from the mixed-effects model for the introductory physics course instructor in the mandatory follow-on physics course because the model did not achieve convergence. Thus, it does not appear that different introductory course faculty types have different effects on follow-on course student achievement. We also again reran the analysis comparing all civilians (with and without prior service experience) to active-duty military faculty to obtain more statistical power. The results of this analysis also did not show any statistically significant differences in teaching effectiveness between faculty types.

Limitations

It is important to note that our analysis of teaching effectiveness is limited in that it does not explore how different types of faculty relate to instructor value-added in courses outside the mandatory introductory core curriculum at USAFA. It is possible that different results would be found in higher-level or more advanced courses that arguably require professors to instill a deeper knowledge of more advanced subjects than the basic concepts that are taught in introductory courses. Given this limitation, it is difficult to come to conclusions regarding the value-added of different faculty types who typically teach these more advanced courses to junior and senior students.

Another limitation is apparent in the very small sample of civilians and civilians with prior service experience who taught the courses examined in this analysis. As shown in Table 5.4, of the introductory math course faculty, there were only 20 instances of civilian faculty members, which were then split into two mutually exclusive groups for modeling. Even when accounting for all types of civilians, this is an extremely small group with which to test for group differences in teaching effectiveness, and further dividing civilian faculty into two separate groups exacerbates this problem. Thus, while we fit a statistical model to ten years of math course data for which the results showed no statistically significant differences in teaching effectiveness across the different faculty types, the reality is that the available data do not provide much statistical power to test for group differences, making the results of this analysis somewhat inconclusive.

While our analysis did not find any systematic statistically significant differences in USAFA student performance as a result of instruction by different types of faculty groups, a prior study using the same USAFA student performance data yielded statistically significant conclusions with regard to the relationship between observable instructor characteristics and instructor value-added. Specifically, research by Carrell and West found that students whose introductory course math instructors tended to be of a lower academic rank, less experienced, or without a doctorate had better scores in the introductory math class, but their scores across the set of follow-on classes were worse when compared with students whose introductory math course instructors were of a higher academic rank, had more teaching experience, and possessed a doctorate.[14] As noted earlier, instructor impact in follow-on courses is considered a better measure of persistent or deeper student learning.

This research is particularly notable given that more experienced, terminal degree–holding instructors of high academic rank are generally found among the civilian faculty, while the active-duty military

[14] Carrell and West, 2010. In the analysis, the authors found a similar pattern of results for all three observable faculty characteristics. However, only academic rank and teaching experience were statistically significant.

faculty members at USAFA are generally characterized by less teaching experience, lower academic rank, and fewer terminal degrees. Although this previous research found that certain observable professor characteristics—which generally correlate strongly with the three types of USAFA faculty considered in this analysis—have a significant relationship with professor value-added, we did not find any systematic differences in the contemporaneous or follow-on course performance of students of the different faculty types.

On the surface, our results may appear to contradict those of Carrell and West, but these separate analyses cannot be directly compared. While we are concerned with whether civilians, civilians with prior service experience, and active-duty military faculty members have a different impact on student learning, Carrell and West were concerned with the correlation between the observable professor characteristics of experience, academic rank, terminal degree attainment, student evaluation ratings, and professor value-added. Differences also persist in the specific data analyzed, our use of triple-nested random effects to control for hierarchical clustering, and the number of modeling steps utilized to determine the correlation between instructor characteristics and value-added. These cumulative differences make a simple comparison of our results to those of Carrell and West problematic. A more detailed discussion of these differences is presented in Appendix E.

Summary

In summary, we did not find consistent, statistically significant differences in teaching effectiveness for introductory courses across the different faculty types after controlling for faculty gender and cadet- and section-level characteristics. However, our small sample size of civilian faculty members, particularly when split into the two categories of civilians and civilians with prior service experience, limited our statistical power to find a significant difference between groups. As a result, our statistical analysis of differences in teaching effectiveness is somewhat inconclusive. Additionally, the cadet survey results reflected only minimal differences in how cadets perceive the influence of faculty groups on their intellectual skill development and in the extent to which different faculty groups bring greater academic depth of knowledge to the classroom. However, USAFA senior leaders and faculty in our focus groups identified civilians as playing a key academic role at USAFA by providing continuity and stability, academic rigor and teaching expertise, connections with broader academia and the research community, and different perspectives compared with military faculty. Furthermore, civilian faculty bring important academic background characteristics to USAFA; the majority of civilian faculty members have doctorates in their academic discipline and greater teaching experience (on average) than active-duty military, and they tend to hold higher academic ranks. Thus, our overall findings suggest that, compared with military faculty, civilian faculty play a particularly critical role in the academic development of cadets.

CHAPTER SIX

Relative Costs of Military and Civilian Faculty

In this chapter, we describe the relative cost to the government of employing an Air Force officer as a faculty member and employing a civilian as a faculty member in terms of cost per individual. We attempted to capture only those costs that differ for military and civilian faculty. Costs associated with base and USAFA infrastructure (e.g., office space, computing resources, supplies) were not included. Therefore, the costs presented here should not be interpreted as an absolute estimate of the total cost of a military or civilian work-year but as a relative cost intended for use in comparing military and civilian faculty.

The costs used in our analysis included both direct compensation paid to the military or civilian faculty member and indirect compensation costs incurred by the government, such as retirement accrual, health insurance, locality adjustments, and relocation expenses. To the extent possible, we obtained costs from published U.S. Department of Defense (DoD) sources or, when those were not available, average actual costs using salary and demographic data provided by USAFA. For example, for military compensation, we used Air Force–specific military composite rates that are published by the Office of the Secretary of Defense; however, civilian faculty compensation rates are USAFA-specific, so we used current salary data to represent average compensation rates. The costs presented here are averaged across military rank (captain/O-3 to colonel/O-6) for military faculty and across civil service rank (which corresponds to academic rank: instructor, assistant professor, associate professor, and professor) for civilian faculty.

In the following sections, we examine the average cost of military faculty and civilian faculty and discuss key considerations regarding the cost estimates.

Military Faculty Costs

Military faculty in the grades of captain through colonel teach at USAFA as a military assignment. These officers hold master's degrees or doctorates in academic disciplines that are taught at USAFA and serve on the academic faculty during their assignment. As part of ensuring that there are enough qualified officers to teach required courses, USAFA also sponsors many of these officers (over 80 percent) in obtaining their advanced academic degrees.

Therefore, our calculations of military faculty costs included the following:

- direct and indirect compensation (e.g., pay, retirement accrual, medical benefits, relocation expenses)
- the cost of obtaining an advanced academic degree.

Compensation

To estimate the annual cost of filling a faculty position with an Air Force officer, we examined compensation paid directly to the officer as well as indirect compensation resulting in costs to the government while the officer serves as a faculty member:

- *Direct compensation* includes basic pay, basic housing allowance, basic subsistence allowance, and incentive, special, and miscellaneous pays.
- *Indirect compensation* includes retirement pay accrual, military-related health care costs financed by the Defense Health Program, permanent-change-of-station costs, Medicare-eligible retiree health care accrual, and the employer portion of the social security tax.

Since estimating these costs can be difficult and assumptions can cause results to vary widely, the Air Force produces standard composite rates that it reports to the Office of the Under Secretary of Defense, Comptroller (OUSD[C]).[1] OUSD(C) publishes military personnel composite standard pay and reimbursement rates annually and mandates that these rates be used "when determining the cost of military personnel for budget/management studies."[2] Table 6.1 lists the composite standard pay and reimbursement rates for the military grades considered in our analysis.

OUSD(C) considers these costs all-inclusive for the purposes of management studies and reimbursement. However, there are additional costs for military personnel, such as accession and training costs and government expenses for Servicemembers' Group Life Insurance

Table 6.1
Military Composite Standard Pay and Reimbursement Rates (FY 2011 $)

Component	Capt (O-3)	Maj (O-4)	Lt Col (O-5)	Col (O-6)
Average basic pay	63,403	78,866	93,313	115,447
Average additional pay/benefits[a]	46,568	50,510	52,784	55,445
Medical costs[b]	10,132	10,132	10,132	10,132
Retirement accrual	20,573	25,590	30,279	37,462
Medicare-eligible retiree health care	5,673	5,673	5,673	5,673
Total cost	146,349	170,771	192,181	224,159

NOTE: FY = fiscal year.

[a] Retirement pay accrual, basic housing allowance, basic subsistence allowance, permanent-change-of-station costs, incentive/special pays, and social security tax.

[b] Medical costs are the average health care costs financed by the Defense Health Program.

1 Air Force Instruction 65-503, *US Air Force Cost and Planning Factors*, February 4, 1994.

2 John P. Roth, deputy comptroller, Office of the Under Secretary of Defense, Comptroller, "FY 2011 Department of Defense (DoD) Military Personnel Composite Standard Pay and Reimbursement Rate," memorandum, March 24, 2010.

(SGLI). We have not included these costs in our analyses for the following reasons:

- Costs associated with service-specific officer acquisition training and initial skills training for officers when they first enter active duty should be amortized over the entire period that the officer serves. Gates and Robbert calculated this cost in 1996 and found that the accession-related costs per work-year for Air Force officers totaled $7,652.[3] The applicability of acquisition, combat, and career field training to military faculty duty in the classroom at USAFA is not directly evident. On-site USAFA training in instructional methods and curriculum development will be more directly applicable to their duties as faculty members. To avoid overstating the annual cost for a military faculty member, we have not included this cost. Note that doing so would increase the final estimate of the annual cost of a military faculty member by more than $7,652.
- Although we included life insurance costs in the civilian portion of the analysis, we chose to not include costs for SGLI in our military faculty calculations. Since the military member currently pays $324 annually in premiums for maximum coverage, and since there is no cost to the government for the insurance payout except in the case of a combat death, the cost to the government is small and difficult to determine.[4]

Advanced Academic Degrees

In addition to compensation costs, there are also potential costs for officers who must earn an advanced academic degree to be qualified to teach at USAFA. Some Air Force officers may have earned a degree at their own expense or through a tuition assistance program qualifying them to teach ("direct hires"). More typically, military faculty mem-

---

[3] Susan M. Gates and Albert A. Robbert, *Comparing the Costs of DoD Military and Civil Service Personnel*, Santa Monica, Calif.: RAND Corporation, MR-980-OSD, 1998.

[4] Secretary of Veterans Affairs, Veterans Benefits Administration, *Servicemembers' and Veterans' Group Life Insurance Handbook*, Washington, D.C., H-29-98-1, revised February 2011.

bers are sent by the Air Force for a master's degree or doctorate prior to teaching at USAFA. They obtain these degrees at a civilian university, the Naval Postgraduate School, or the Air Force Institute of Technology (AFIT) in residence; these officers are said to be "USAFA pipeline faculty." The costs for obtaining an advanced academic degree include tuition and fees, temporary duty (TDY) expenses, AFIT Civilian Institute Programs (CI) oversight costs, and compensation costs while a student.

We obtained data on the average cost of tuition and fees from AFIT/CI for military officers who attended master's degree programs in FYs 2007–2009 and graduated in FYs 2008–2010 and who attended doctoral programs in FYs 2006–2007 and graduated in FYs 2009–2010. Tuition costs can vary widely depending on the degree program, the university attended, and the availability of scholarship dollars. For this data set, the highest master's degree cost was $61,000 and the minimum cost was $0 (cost covered by scholarship); the highest doctoral degree cost was $114,000 and the minimum cost was $11,000. The average tuition cost used in this analysis also includes 20 USAFA faculty pipeline students who attended AFIT in residence during the same time frame as those in the data set. The AFIT Office of Financial Management uses a standard per-credit-hour rate of $333,[5] with most master's programs at AFIT requiring 60 credit hours and doctoral programs requiring the equivalent of 108 credit hours for a total tuition cost of $19,980 and $35,964, respectively.

In addition to tuition costs, all AFIT students (in residence and at civilian universities) are afforded the opportunity to attend certain approved conferences in support of their degree programs. AFIT/CI reports an average TDY cost of nearly $500 for each master's degree student and just over $1,000 for each doctoral student.

There are also oversight costs for the AFIT/CI program office. While attending civilian schools, USAFA pipeline students are assigned to AFIT/CI, which has oversight of their degree program, disperses funds for their tuition and fees, assists with issues associated with living away from a military installation, and ensures that students continue to

---

[5] The AFIT in-residence per-credit-hour rate was provided by AFIT/CI.

meet their commitments as Air Force officers (e.g., completing required training and physical fitness testing). To perform this oversight function, AFIT/CI currently employs eight civilians (a mix of civil service and contract personnel) with an estimated operating budget of at least $480,000 per year. Given that the average annual number of students managed by AFIT/CI is 650, the average annual cost for each USAFA pipeline faculty student is $738. USAFA faculty pipeline students constitute approximately 18 percent (an average of 117 per year) of this group's workload.

Finally, military personnel receive the same direct and indirect compensation described earlier while in their degree programs. Therefore, we used the same military personnel composite standard pay and reimbursement rates for FYs 2007–2010 that were presented in Table 6.1 to calculate compensation costs for students in degree programs.

For this analysis, we amortized the total costs of obtaining these degrees over the period the officer serves in his or her faculty position *and* over the period he or she serves in subsequent Air Force positions requiring that degree. Reviewing ten years of Air Force officer career data, we summed the time served in positions requiring a doctorate or master's for those who earned a degree for the purpose of teaching at USAFA. Since it is unusual for an O-6 to be sent for a pipeline master's degree, the post-degree utilization rates for O-6s are based on a very small sample size and therefore are not reliable, so we did not use them in our analysis. To the degree that faculty with the designation of Senior Military Professor have been present on the USAFA faculty over the past ten years, they were also included in the utilization rates.

Tables 6.2 and 6.3 show the average total costs associated with obtaining a degree. These rates are based on an average of 17 months to complete a master's degree and 36 months to complete a doctorate.[6] Note that we did not attempt to account for officers who were promoted during their graduate studies (doing so would increase the total cost of the degree).

---

[6] We calculated the average time for degree completion from actual start and graduation dates for 65 doctoral students and 83 master's students between FY 2006 and FY 2010. These data were provided by AFIT/CI.

Table 6.2
Total and Amortized Cost of a USAFA Pipeline Master's Degree (FY 2011 $)

Cost	Capt (O-3)	Maj (O-4)	Lt Col (O-5)	Col (O-6)
Average tuition and fees	18,114	18,114	18,114	18,114
Average TDY expenses	479	479	479	479
AFIT/CI management cost	1,044	1,044	1,044	1,044
Compensation	203,000	237,284	267,660	310,180
Total cost of degree	222,637	256,921	287,297	329,817
Degree utilization (years)	5.460	3.622	3.511	Small sample
Amortized annual degree cost	40,773	70,926	81,830	

Table 6.3
Total and Amortized Cost of a USAFA Pipeline Doctoral Degree (FY 2011 $)

Cost	Capt (O-3)	Maj (O-4)	Lt Col (O-5)	Col (O-6)
Average tuition and fees	34,275	34,275	34,275	34,275
Average TDY expenses	1,015	1,015	1,015	1,015
AFIT/CI management cost	2,210	2,210	2,210	2,210
Compensation	411,133	489,134	552,087	639,720
Total cost of degree	448,633	526,634	589,587	677,220
Degree utilization (years)	4.471	4.393	4.928	6.373
Amortized annual degree cost	100,348	119,888	119,631	106,271

An important observation from this review of military faculty costs is that the total average cost of a degree is driven primarily by the cost of compensation for the officer during the time he or she is attending the degree program. Even in the case of an O-3 obtaining a master's degree, tuition and fees amount to only 8.1 percent of the total cost of sending that officer to school.

Some would argue that the pay and allowances for officers in pipeline degree programs should not be counted in comparing officer and civilian faculty costs. Total Air Force officer strength is set before its component parts, including an STP account (students, transients, patients, and prisoners), are sized. Thus, total pay and allowances for the officer force are unaffected by the number of officers in degree programs. We believe this is only partially true because, in the long run, changes in the size of the STP account can affect programmed officer end strength. Further, there is an opportunity cost related to the time officers spend in a pipeline degree program: the value of the officers' service lost to other missions in the Air Force. We chose to carry through all the relative costs to the government of employing an Air Force officer for the following reasons:

- Our analysis focused on ensuring the success of USAFA as a stand-alone organization.
- In discussions with Air Force senior leaders and USAFA leadership, the argument was raised repeatedly that either military or civilian faculty were more cost-effective, and our goal was to show how the two compared.
- In a drawdown environment, at a time when reductions in the number of officer positions are required, it is prudent to examine areas in which reductions in military presence are cost-effective.
- Amortizing the cost of officer pay and allowances for those in the education pipeline into the cost of military faculty monetizes the opportunity cost and provides a more complete comparison of the costs of military and civilian faculty.

Thus, our cost analysis provides a basis for discussing the relative costs of military and civilian USAFA faculty.

Total Annual Costs

Using the costs in Tables 6.1, 6.2, and 6.3, Table 6.4 summarizes the average annual costs for a military faculty member at USAFA.

Table 6.4
Average Annual Cost of a USAFA Military Faculty Member (FY 2011 $)

Military Faculty Type	Capt (O-3)	Maj (O-4)	Lt Col (O-5)	Col (O-6)
Direct hire, no pipeline degree required	146,349	170,771	192,181	224,159
Pipeline master's degree required	187,122	241,697	274,011	364,303
Pipeline doctorate required	246,697	290,659	311,812	330,430

Civilian Faculty Costs

USAFA civilian faculty members are on an administratively determined (AD) pay schedule that is similar to the general schedule pay scale but allows for academic-specific duty titles and alternate pay settings to ensure that USAFA can attract high-quality faculty.[7] USAFA faculty are designated AD-21 for instructors through AD-24 for full professors. Our calculations of civilian faculty costs included the following components:

- direct and indirect compensation (e.g., pay, retirement accrual, medical benefits)
- cost to advertise, hire, and relocate.

Compensation

Civilian faculty members at USAFA, like all civil service workers, receive both wage and nonwage compensation ("benefits"). For the purposes of this study, we collected wage data for current USAFA civilian faculty members (185 personnel), including their duty title, basic salary rate, and locality adjustment (adjustment to the basic rate based on duty location). It is important to note that civilian salary rates differ depending on the academic discipline. The overall average civilian faculty total annual salary across all academic ranks was $96,517. Engineering Mechanics Department faculty had the highest average total

[7] Our analysis did not include USAFA's endowed chairs.

salary ($131,020), and language faculty had the lowest ($69,884). For our purposes, we used the average civilian faculty salary within academic rank across all academic specialties to make easier comparisons with military faculty costs. Table 6.5 shows average wage compensation for USAFA civilian faculty by academic rank.

Table 6.5
Average Wage Compensation for Current USAFA Civilian Faculty (FY 2011 $)

Compensation	Instructor (AD-21)	Assistant Professor (AD-22)	Associate Professor (AD-23)	Professor (AD-24)
Average basic salary	56,315	75,605	91,030	105,428
Average locality adjustment	7,974	10,706	12,890	14,928
Total average salary	64,289	86,311	103,920	120,356

Nonwage compensation is more difficult to determine and, at times, open to interpretation. Therefore, we sought internal guidance on how to calculate this compensation. In 2008, the Office of Management and Budget (OMB) published cost factors for use in decisions regarding the outsourcing of federal activities to the private sector.[8] These cost factors express the value of certain federal benefits as a percentage of salary. Table 6.6 shows the cost factors from the 2008 OMB memorandum.

The insurance and health benefit includes the costs of life insurance (0.2 percent of salary) and health insurance (6.8 percent). This factor is based on actuarial estimates for the costs of the government-paid portion of health insurance under the Federal Employees Health Benefits Plan and the Federal Employees Government Life Insurance program and excludes the employee-paid portion of health insurance. This figure is multiplied by the average participation rates and divided

8 Jim Nussle, director, Office of Management and Budget, "Update to Civilian Position Full Fringe Benefit Cost Factor, Federal Pay Raise Assumptions, and Inflation Factors used in OMB Circular No. A-76, 'Performance of Commercial Activities,'" Washington, D.C.: Office of Management and Budget, M-08-13, March 11, 2008.

Table 6.6
Components of Civilian Full Fringe Benefit Cost

Benefit	Cost Factor (%)
Insurance and health benefit	7.0
Standard civilian retirement benefit	26.1
Medicare benefit	1.45
Miscellaneous fringe benefit	1.7
Total civilian position full fringe benefits	36.25

by the average civilian employee's salary to derive a factor as a percentage of basic salary.

The standard civilian retirement benefit includes the annual accrual cost for pension benefits, including social security, the defined-contribution Thrift Savings Plan, the defined-benefit Federal Employees Retirement System or Civil Service Retirement System, and the accrual cost for postretirement health benefits. It excludes the employee-paid portion of retirement. This cost represents the "normal cost" of each program—the value of the pension compensation in a given year.

Finally, the Medicare benefit includes the percentage of the employer's share of the Medicare payroll tax. The miscellaneous fringe benefit category includes payments for workers' compensation, unemployment premiums, bonuses, and certain types of employee awards.

Given that, as of March 2011, 42 percent of USAFA's permanent civilian faculty members had prior service experience, it is likely that the percentages in Table 6.6 are overstated. For example, military retirees would not incur the same medical costs as nonretiree civilians, since they would most likely use military retiree medical benefits as their primary health benefit. USAFA estimates that, in fact, their average civilian employee total fringe benefit is 26.5 percent of salary.[9] However, to ensure that all potential costs are accounted for, we used OMB's 36.25 percent for our analysis.

[9] Information obtained from USAFA, April 28, 2011.

Cost of Advertising, Hiring, Relocation, and Sabbatical

In estimating civilian faculty costs, an additional factor to consider is the cost to advertise, hire, and relocate civilian faculty. USAFA estimates that the average cost to hire a single faculty member is $33,400 ($2,400 for advertising the vacancy in academic publications, $6,000 in travel expenses for interviewing multiple candidates, and $25,000 in moving/relocation costs for the newly hired faculty member). For each faculty member, we spread this cost over his or her tenure at USAFA. The average tenure for a civilian faculty member at USAFA is difficult to approximate due to the increase in the number of civilian faculty hired in recent years. The 2008–2011 average retention rate of 96.4 percent suggests a tenure of nearly 28 years;[10] however, for the purposes of this analysis, we used a more conservative ten-year tenure to ensure that all potential costs were included.[11]

Civilian faculty members are normally eligible for an initial six-month USAFA-supported sabbatical during the seventh year of employment. These sabbaticals allow faculty members to participate in a variety of professional development opportunities.[12] These absences are normally at the staffing expense of the academic department, so there is a cost associated with sabbaticals, since civilian faculty serve 78 months in the classroom for every 84 months they are paid. Annualized, this equates to serving approximately 11.14 months per year. We added the cost to replace the faculty member during his or her sabbatical (presumably with a temporary hire) to the annual cost of a civilian faculty member.

Total Annual Costs

Table 6.7 shows the total annual cost to the government for the employment of a civilian faculty member at USAFA.

---

[10] Information provided by USAFA, 2011.

[11] This ten-year estimate is derived from information provided by USAFA, 2011. We used ten years rather than 28 years to ensure that we did not underestimate the costs of advertising, hiring, and relocating newly hired civilian faculty.

[12] U.S. Air Force Academy Faculty Operating Instruction 36-179, *Civilian Faculty Sabbatical Program*, December 21, 2010.

Table 6.7
Average Annual Cost of a USAFA Civilian Faculty Member (FY 2011 $)

Compensation	Instructor (AD-21)	Assistant Professor (AD-22)	Associate Professor (AD-23)	Professor (AD-24)
Total salary	64,289	86,311	103,920	120,356
Full fringe benefit	23,305	31,288	37,671	43,629
Advertising, hiring, relocation and sabbatical	8,542	10,236	11,591	12,855
Total average annual cost	96,136	127,835	153,181	176,840

Summary

Figure 6.1 presents our estimates of annual costs for military and civilian faculty members. In general, a military faculty member is more

Figure 6.1
Total Average Annual Cost of Military and Civilian Faculty

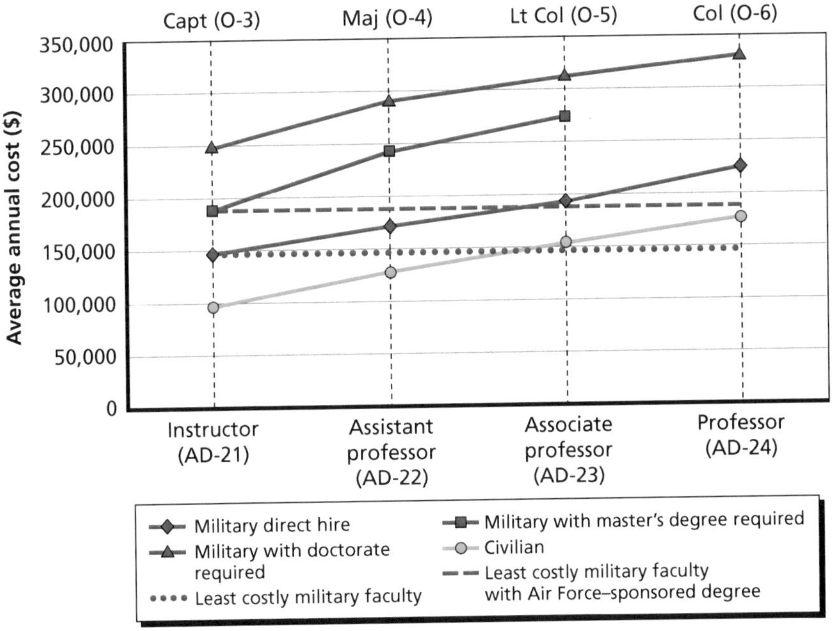

RAND *MG1237-6.1*

expensive, even when a pipeline degree is not required. In Figure 6.1, the dotted line illustrates that the least expensive military faculty member (captain/O-3, direct hire) is more expensive than a civilian instructor or assistant professor and approximately equal to an associate professor. As the figure shows, if an Air Force officer is sent for any level of pipeline degree, the cost of that military faculty member is more than the average cost of the highest-ranking civilian professor.

Further Areas for Consideration

During the course of this analysis, it was evident that several factors that we did not consider may affect decisions about the appropriate mix of military and civilian faculty at USAFA:

- *Future utilization.* In our analysis, we amortized the costs of military faculty obtaining a USAFA pipeline degree over the utilization of that degree for Air Force requirements. It is more cost-effective to send military faculty for degrees that are most likely to be of further use in the Air Force beyond their tenure at USAFA. For example, it is likely more advantageous to the Air Force to send an officer for an electrical engineering degree than for an English degree. In addition, USAFA's plans to increase the number of faculty members with the designation of Senior Military Professor may increase post-degree utilization and reduce the annual cost of military faculty.[13]
- *Direct hires.* Given the high costs of sending military faculty members for degrees, increased attention should be paid to finding and assigning military personnel with the required degree to USAFA. Over the past several years, AFPC has made increasing efforts to seek out individuals with the required degrees; however, functional areas and assignment officers must be willing to give up these assets to USAFA, and USAFA must be willing to accept

[13] The plan to add more senior military professors was articulated in a meeting with Dean of Faculty Brig Gen Dana Born and department heads on August 2, 2011; the intention was to increase the number of senior military professors from 14 to 62 over the next several years. Further information about senior military professors can be found in HQ United States Air Force Academy Instruction 36-3520, 2010.

faculty with these degrees. Holding the number of USAFA military faculty constant at current levels but reducing the number of new degree starts allotted to USAFA each year should result in an increase in direct hires and in second- or third-tour USAFA military faculty. While this outcome may be more cost-effective, USAFA has expressed a need for recently earned or "fresh degrees," especially in technical specialties. Clearly there are trade-offs to be considered.

- *Availability in the classroom.* We addressed annual costs in our analysis; however, we could expect a difference in the average number of days in the classroom for military and civilian faculty. Military personnel earn a total of 30 days of leave per year. They do not earn sick leave but are given time off for illness as required. Personnel may also be required to attend additional training during their time at USAFA, such as Squadron Officer School. In addition, military faculty may deploy; statements reflect that, in 2009, an average of 60 military faculty members (16 percent) were absent due to deployments.[14] Civilians, on the other hand, earn 13–26 days of leave per year, depending on their years of federal service, and 13 days of sick leave, bringing the total to fewer than 40 days per year. Further analysis may show that there are costs inherent in the number of days faculty are absent from the classroom (e.g., sabbaticals), at times requiring the hiring of temporary civilian faculty.

---

[14] U.S. House of Representatives, 2009.

CHAPTER SEVEN

Faculty Staffing Challenges

The Air Force is having difficulty meeting USAFA military faculty staffing requirements. We explored this issue by gathering information from several sources, including interviews with USAFA senior leaders and staff in charge of faculty staffing, as well as focus groups with current faculty members.[1] We also conducted a daylong information session with the AFPC personnel who are specifically responsible for USAFA military assignments and a selected number of representatives from officer assignment teams to gather additional information on assignment policies and practices and the challenges AFPC faces with regard to USAFA staffing. This chapter focuses primarily on military staffing challenges, given that this was the primary issue identified in our research. However, we do include a brief discussion of civilian staffing challenges at the end of the chapter.

Military Staffing Challenges

Headquartered at Randolph Air Force Base in Texas, AFPC is responsible for working with USAFA to assign qualified officers to teach as members of the faculty. USAFA staffing requirements are filled through three sources. The first is the advanced academic degree faculty pipeline, which consists of officers who have been sponsored by USAFA to obtain a degree and are then required to do a payback teaching tour.

[1] See Appendix B for more details on the methodology.

Tours are generally three years for a master's degree and four years for a doctorate. However, in some cases, these tours can be extended to meet USAFA's needs. The second faculty staffing source is a smaller pipeline program called the Graduate School Program, which sends a small number of highly qualified USAFA cadets directly to advanced academic degree programs upon graduation. These former cadets are also required to complete a payback teaching tour at USAFA after receiving their degree. The third source consists of officers found through the normal assignment system. These are officers who have not been directly sponsored for a degree but hold the required advanced academic degree and are selected to teach at USAFA. Generally, these officers are used to fill billets that cannot be satisfied through the first two staffing sources.

Although there are three sources designed to meet USAFA's military faculty staffing needs, both AFPC and USAFA personnel identified several key challenges to meeting the requirements:

- officers' lack of advanced academic degrees
- assignment prioritization and staffing requirements
- misalignment with career paths and negative perceptions of USAFA teaching duty
- officer deployments
- loss of funding for temporary faculty.

Lack of Advanced Academic Degrees

First, both AFPC and USAFA identified one of the primary challenges as finding military officers with the required advanced academic degrees, particularly doctorates. Most officers obtain master's degrees at some point in their careers (though not necessarily in a discipline needed on the USAFA faculty), but fewer officers obtain doctorates without direct sponsorship. Even with a pipeline of officers sponsored for degrees, the timing of obtaining the degree, conflicts with career paths, and other assignment policies often result in a very small pool of qualified officers available for faculty duty.

Finding officers with the appropriate advanced academic degree is also more difficult for some academic disciplines than for others. For those academic disciplines that are aligned with an Air Force specialty or are highly utilized in the Air Force, such as engineering, finding military faculty members is not as problematic. However, for those academic departments that do not align directly with an Air Force specialty, such as English or philosophy, the only officers with the required advanced degrees may be those who were directly sponsored by USAFA. Therefore, finding military faculty members who are qualified to teach in these disciplines can be very difficult. As one department head commented,

> We just don't have bodies out there that have a master's degree in English that we can go pull in here to teach, and at the same time, you want a little quality control too. You don't just want anybody coming in here. You want to interview them and make sure they are going to fit and make sure that they have the requisite skills.

Thus, finding officers with the required advanced academic degree to teach at USAFA is a continuing challenge. This challenge is further exacerbated when there is a desire for officers with doctorates or degrees in disciplines that do not directly align with an Air Force specialty.

Assignment Prioritizations and Staffing Requirements

A second factor contributing to military faculty staffing challenges at USAFA is how billets are prioritized across the Air Force. Overall, assignment priorities are driven by three factors: (1) Air Force mission needs, (2) officer professional development paths, and (3) individual officer preferences. Therefore, as with most other units, when taking into account the prioritization of certain billets (such as joint billets), as well as officers who are deployed, the overall percentage of officers available to serve a USAFA faculty assignment is already greatly reduced—and the number qualified to do so is even smaller. Therefore, with a limited number of officers to fill assignments across the Air Force, most officers who do have the appropriate advanced academic degree are likely to get assigned to other billets prior to USAFA. In particular, Air Force shortages of rated officers, scientists, and engineers make it difficult for USAFA to pull such individuals out of their normal career paths for further academic development and a follow-on teaching assignment.

Misalignment with Career Paths and Negative Perceptions of USAFA Teaching Duty

Representatives from officer assignment teams also identified challenges in pulling officers from their primary career fields to obtain advanced academic degrees and then teach at USAFA. Each career field has a designated path for officer professional development that includes meeting certain professional and educational requirements, obtaining operational experience, and holding command positions. Because teaching at USAFA requires officers to be removed from their primary career path for a certain amount of time, representatives from officer assignment teams reported difficulty in ensuring that these officers did not fall behind their peers in terms of their professional development. In some cases, such as for pilots, completing an immediate payback tour at USAFA following a degree can also be particularly difficult due to mission requirements for rated officers. As a result, AFPC officer assignment teams are often cautious of releasing officers to obtain an advanced degree or teach at USAFA, particularly when they have an unfilled billet designated as a higher priority. This cautiousness is further increased when there is a risk that USAFA may request to keep the officer and send him or her to a doctoral program followed by another instructor tour.

Consistent with these challenges, USAFA senior leaders and faculty members in our focus groups expressed frustration with their ability to sponsor officers for degrees and get them sent back to teach at USAFA. In the words of one faculty member,

> It's really challenging on the military side to find someone who is qualified academically. We certainly want someone who will have a master's degree in the area, at least, preferably a doctorate, but that's pretty rare. So, it's really hard to find people, and then it is hard to get people released to come teach or to send them off to go get advanced degrees to eventually come teach—really, really challenging.

Similarly, another stated, "We can barely fill master's or doctorate billets, and not with the quality faculty we could 15 years ago. The Air Force will not release people."

Related to this point, respondents also described the perception in the Air Force that serving at USAFA, particularly for an extended period, can hurt career advancement opportunities. For example, according to one department head,

> This is no longer an assignment that is valued by the United States Air Force in a variety of career fields. I have junior officers that have been told by more-senior officers, "Do not go to the Academy. It is not in your interest, and it is detrimental to your career to teach."

Similarly, when discussing the problem of getting junior faculty to return for a second teaching tour, a military faculty member said, "If they want to have the opportunity to make O-6 when they are an O-4, they may not choose to go that academic track, and we may have lost the best talent in our department that way."[2]

Since we completed our data collection, the Air Force Chief of Staff issued a memorandum in March 2012 stating, "We must capitalize on the expertise and leadership of our very best Airmen by placing them in critical training and education instructor roles across the Air Force." The memo stated that "a successful career should include a tour of duty as an instructor."[3] Thus, some of the issues and negative perceptions related to getting officers assigned to teach at USAFA may lessen in the future.

Officer Deployments and Loss of Funding for Temporary Faculty

As a result of the issues outlined here, USAFA reported often facing empty military faculty billets across departments, with officer deployments further contributing to understaffing. To fill these positions,

---

[2] We discuss the issue of the impact of USAFA teaching duty on officers' advancement potential in more detail in Chapter Eight.

[3] Gen Norton A. Schwartz, Chief of Staff, U.S. Air Force, "Instructor Duty—Building Leaders Is Everybody's Business," memorandum, March 8, 2012.

USAFA has relied on National Guard and reserve members or hired temporary civilian faculty. However, at the time of our research, funding for both National Guard and reserve members and temporary hires was being reduced due to budget limitations. As a result, USAFA representatives expressed concern that it would become even more difficult to fill faculty positions in the future.

Civilian Staffing Challenges

USAFA senior leaders and faculty also noted some difficulties related to civilian hiring. However, these challenges were reported as minimal compared with finding qualified military faculty and seemed to vary across departments. USAFA staff reported that the most common challenge in finding civilian faculty members was faculty fit with the USAFA culture. For example, unlike most universities, USAFA expects its professors to be present in their offices and available to cadets for the majority of the workday. There is also a strong focus on military training, limited governance roles, and no tenure system. As a result, teaching at USAFA may not be a good fit for some civilian academics.

Consistent with recent concerns regarding hiring civilians who would bring an outside perspective, civilian faculty members in our focus groups also expressed concern that there was a preference for civilian faculty with prior military experience in hiring; this was rarely mentioned by prior-service civilian faculty members or active-duty military faculty members, however. This concern about prior-service personnel composing a large percentage of the civilian faculty population has been raised before. For example, a 2010 report from the House Armed Services Committee, Subcommittee on Oversight and Investigation, found that "USAFA has not done enough to hire pure civilian faculty."[4] In response, USAFA senior leaders argued that the civilian hiring process tries not to "advantage military or disadvantage military, retired military."[5] However, it also argued that prior-service personnel

---

[4] U.S. House of Representatives, 2010, p. 127.

[5] Born, 2009, p. 25.

provide a beneficial balance of military experience and advanced scholarship that is not possible with purely civilian faculty.

Summary

USAFA currently faces difficulties in filling its military faculty positions for a range of reasons: a limited number of officers with the required advanced academic degrees, staff allocation plans for the broader Air Force that often prioritize other billets, misalignment with career paths, and fewer officers due to deployments. Additionally, due to budget limitations, funding for temporary faculty to fill these empty positions is also being reduced. USAFA reported considerably less difficulty in finding qualified civilian faculty. However, due to the unique nature of USAFA culture, not all civilians will be interested in teaching at the Academy.

CHAPTER EIGHT

Officer Career Development

The final factor that we examined as part of this research was officer career development, which we define as the impact that USAFA instructor duty has on the professional development of officers sent to teach at USAFA. We examined the impact on officer career development through our interviews and focus groups with USAFA senior leaders and faculty, as well as in discussions with AFPC personnel who were responsible for the career progression of officers.[1] We also examined whether USAFA instructor duty affects officer promotion rates.

Interview and Focus Group Findings

As described in Chapter Three, USAFA senior leaders argued that USAFA produces a "second graduating class" of officers who are sponsored for advanced academic degrees and assigned to teach at the Academy. This was particularly discussed in reference to the junior rotating officers who serve at USAFA. Specifically, they argued that a faculty tour provides an opportunity for officers to further develop their strategic thinking and gain greater expertise in their respective disciplines. This experience then ostensibly benefits the broader Air Force when these officers return to their primary career fields and is especially beneficial when there is a direct alignment between the USAFA academic department in which they teach and their Air Force specialty

[1] See Appendix B for details on the methodology.

(e.g., engineering). Similar arguments have been made at the other service academies. For example, USMA often highlights the instructor duty positions held by General David Petraeus and General Martin Dempsey earlier in their careers. Thus, USAFA argues, having military faculty members benefits not only the officer development of cadets but also the professional development of officers assigned to teach there—and, ultimately, the broader U.S. Air Force.

Despite the potential positive impact of this second graduating class on officer career development, findings from our faculty focus groups indicate that there is a perception in the broader Air Force that teaching at USAFA is not a valued assignment and can even damage an officer's career. Consistent with this perspective, our discussions with the AFPC personnel who are responsible for officers' professional development indicated that faculty tours at USAFA do not always fit designated career paths. As mentioned in Chapter Seven, representatives from officer assignment teams described how each career field has a designated path for officer professional development that includes meeting certain professional and educational requirements, obtaining operational experience, and holding command positions. To teach at USAFA, officers are often taken out of their primary career field to go obtain an advanced academic degree and then fulfill a three- to four-year tour at USAFA. Because teaching at USAFA requires officers to be removed from their primary career path for a certain amount of time, representatives from officer assignment teams reported difficulty in ensuring that these officers did not fall behind their peers in terms of their professional development.

This situation is particularly challenging when officers obtain both a master's degree and doctorate and complete two payback teaching tours at USAFA. Officer assignment team members indicated that these officers are often especially behind their peers who have gained operational and command experience and have had the time to meet other professional development requirements. As an illustration, Figure 8.1 shows two potential tracks to obtaining a master's degree and doctorate, including required faculty tours as payback for the degrees.

The first track shown in the figure represents the fastest way to earn a master's degree and doctorate and to complete the subsequent

Figure 8.1
Two Potential Tracks to Degree Attainment and USAFA Tour Completion and Their Impact on Promotion

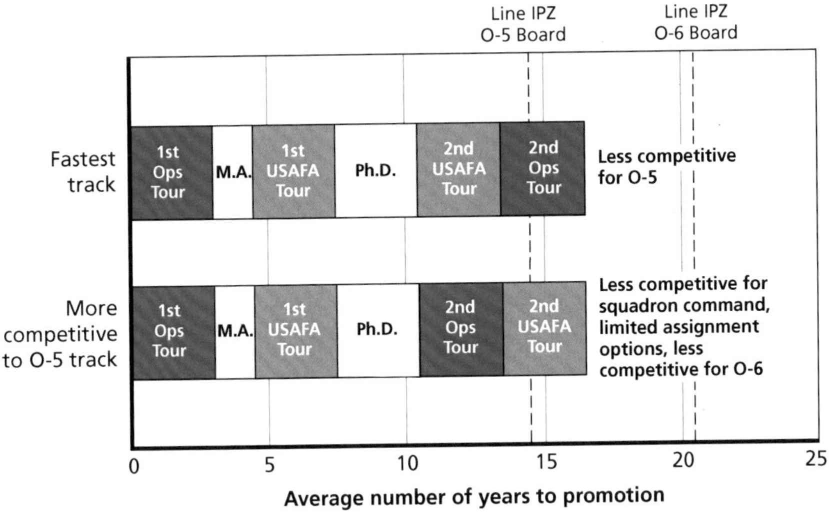

NOTE: "Line" refers to the career field grouping for most officers. IPZ = in the promotion zone.
RAND *MG1237-8.1*

payback tours at USAFA. However, officers that take this track are likely less competitive for promotion to lieutenant colonel/O-5, primarily because the majority of the officer's career has been spent as a student or faculty member. This is in contrast to peers who would have had more opportunities to gain operational experience. The second track presented in the figure provides a more competitive track for promotion to lieutenant colonel/O-5 given an intervening operational tour immediately after completing the doctorate. However, officers following this track are likely still less competitive for promotion to colonel/O-6 for the same reasons, including being less likely to have command opportunities. As a military faculty member stated during our focus groups,

> I totally counsel all of my captains and majors we send for doctorates that you realize what this does . . . but I understand the Air Force perspective completely. It's three years out of an operational

job. . . . I get it, I mean, I only have ten years of operational experience, not 20 like someone else in my year group.

Thus, although USAFA argues that teaching duty provides a beneficial experience for officers, spending a significant amount of time outside their core career field and missing key opportunities for command experience would appear to have a negative impact on future advancement.

Differences in Promotion Rates

To explore the issue of officer professional development in more detail, we examined officer promotion rates to assess whether USAFA tours—and when these tours occur during officers' careers—affect career advancement. Specifically, we examined promotions to major/O-4, lieutenant colonel/O-5, and colonel/O-6 for FYs 2001–2011 for the following four groups:

1. officers who had never taught at USAFA
2. officers who taught at USAFA only as company-grade officers
3. officers who taught at USAFA only as field-grade officers
4. officers who taught at USAFA as both company-grade officers and field-grade officers.

These categories allowed us to examine the impact of teaching tours at USAFA and the importance of the timing of these tours during officers' careers.

As an initial point of comparison, we examined three sets of historical IPZ rates: promotion to major/O-4, lieutenant colonel/O-5, and colonel/O-6.[2] These promotion rates are shown in Figure 8.2. The first (blue) bars in each set in the figure indicate average IPZ promotion board rates, or the percentage of all officers who are promoted to O-4,

---

[2] We opted to concentrate on IPZ promotions because the majority of officers are promoted in the promotion zone; relatively fewer officers are promoted below or above the promotion zone.

Figure 8.2
Comparison of IPZ Promotion Rates for Military Faculty, by USAFA Teaching Tour Type

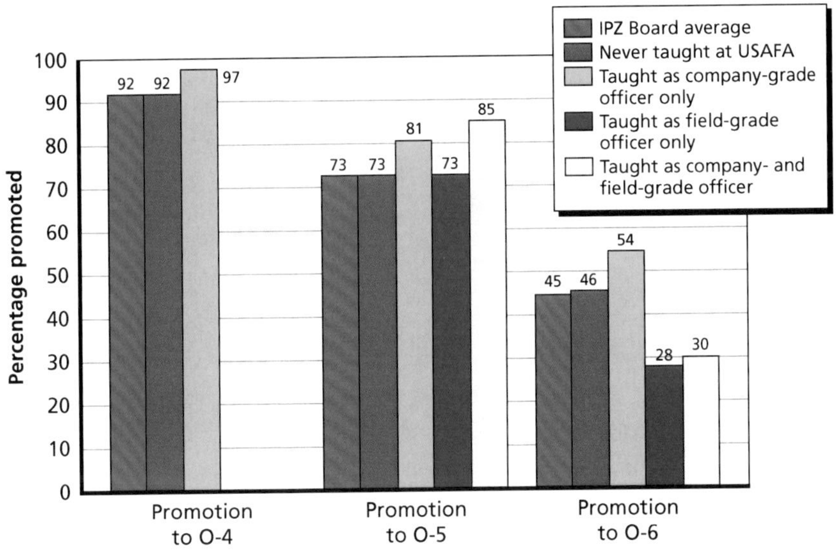

RAND *MG1237-8.2*

O-5, and O-6, respectively. In each set, the second (red) bar indicates the corresponding promotion rate for officers who have never taught at USAFA, the third (green) bar represents officers who taught at USAFA as company-grade officers only, the fourth (purple) represents officers who taught as field-grade officers only, and the fifth (light blue) represents officers who taught as both company-grade officers and field-grade officers.

As shown in Figure 8.2, officers who taught at USAFA as company-grade officers only were promoted to O-4, O-5, and O-6 at rates above the board average and above the average for officers who never taught at USAFA. Furthermore, they were much more likely to be promoted to colonel/O-6 than both of the other USAFA faculty groups (field-grade officer only and company-grade and field-grade officer). Thus, these officers seem to outperform their peers, and as expected, their career advancement does not seem to have been negatively affected by a USAFA teaching tour.

The promotion rate of officers who taught at USAFA as field-grade officers only was consistent with the board average for promotion to lieutenant colonel/O-5 but below the board average and below the rate for officers who never taught at USAFA for promotion to colonel/O-6. Our qualitative findings indicate that this lower rate of promotion is likely due to missed opportunities for command experience while a field-grade officer, which is particularly important for promotion to colonel/O-6.

Finally, the results show that officers who taught at USAFA as company-grade officers and again as field-grade officers were promoted to lieutenant colonel/O-5 above the board average and above the average of all other USAFA faculty groups, even those who served as company-grade officers only. However, when it came to promotion to colonel O-6, for which command experience is critical, they were promoted at rates below the board average, below that of officers who had never taught at USAFA, and below that of officers who taught as company-grade officers only.

Consistent with these descriptive findings regarding differences in basic promotion rates, regression analyses indicate that officers who taught at USAFA as company-grade officers only were significantly more likely to be promoted to O-4, O-5, and O-6 than officers who had never taught at USAFA. Officers who taught as field-grade officers only were just as likely to be promoted to O-5 as officers who never taught at USAFA but significantly less likely to be promoted to O-6. Finally, officers who taught as both company-grade officers and field-grade officers were significantly more likely to be promoted to O-5 than officers who never taught at USAFA but significantly less likely to be promoted to O-6.

However, after controlling for officers' career histories (e.g., education, key assignments, and command experience), in all cases, associations between the USAFA tour types and promotion are weaker in magnitude and no longer statistically significant.[3] For example, offi-

---

[3] The one exception is officers who served at USAFA as company-grade officers only. This group was still significantly more likely to be promoted to O-6 than officers who never taught at USAFA.

cers who taught as field-grade officers only are significantly less likely to be promoted to colonel/O-6 than those who have never taught at USAFA. However, this association is no longer statistically significant when controlling for career history. Thus, the regression results provide further support for our descriptions of how acquiring advanced degrees and teaching at USAFA as field-grade officers can interfere with officers' career development.

In conclusion, both the descriptive and regression results suggest that sending officers to teach one tour as company-grade officers is the least likely to have a negative impact on future career advancement. This is also the best way to have a successful second graduation class of officers who will become future senior leaders in the Air Force.

Current Alignment of Manpower Grade Authorizations and Assignments

As described in Chapter Two, although manpower grade authorizations designate the majority of USAFA academic faculty billets for company-grade officers, there is currently a misalignment between officer assignments and USAFA manpower grade authorizations. As Figure 8.3 shows, company-grade officers are currently understaffed while lieutenant colonels/O-5s are overstaffed at USAFA. Further, as Figure 8.4 shows, this misalignment has only increased over the past two decades.

Company-grade officers are not understaffed across the Air Force, however. In fact, when we look at the Air Force as a whole, there are enough company-grade officers to meet all company-grade authorizations. Thus, other factors contribute to the misalignment at USAFA. First, as described earlier, the timing of obtaining advanced degrees and serving in a faculty position at USAFA does not always fit easily into officers' designated career paths. Therefore, officers who have been sponsored for a master's degree may not be sent to complete their payback tours until they become field-grade officers. Similarly, a majority of officers who are sponsored to get a doctorate have served at USAFA on a prior tour. As shown in Figure 8.1 earlier in this chapter, these offi-

Figure 8.3
Alignment of Manpower Grade Authorizations and USAFA Military Faculty Assignments

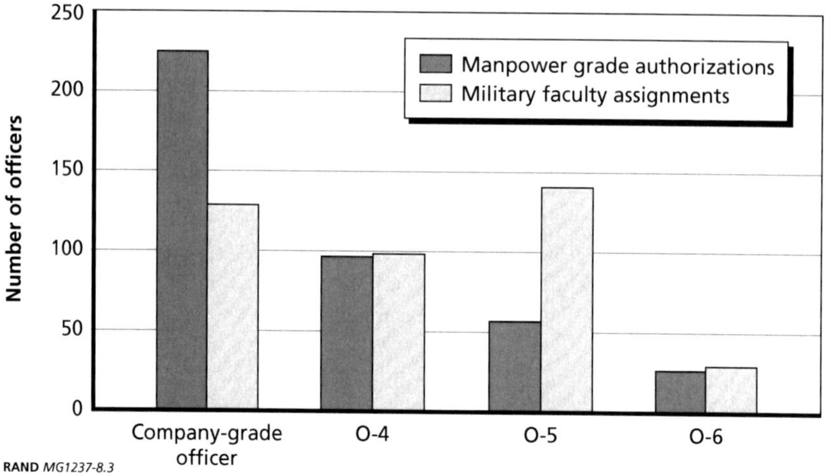

RAND *MG1237-8.3*

Figure 8.4
Alignment of Manpower Grade Authorizations and USAFA Military Faculty Assignments Over Time

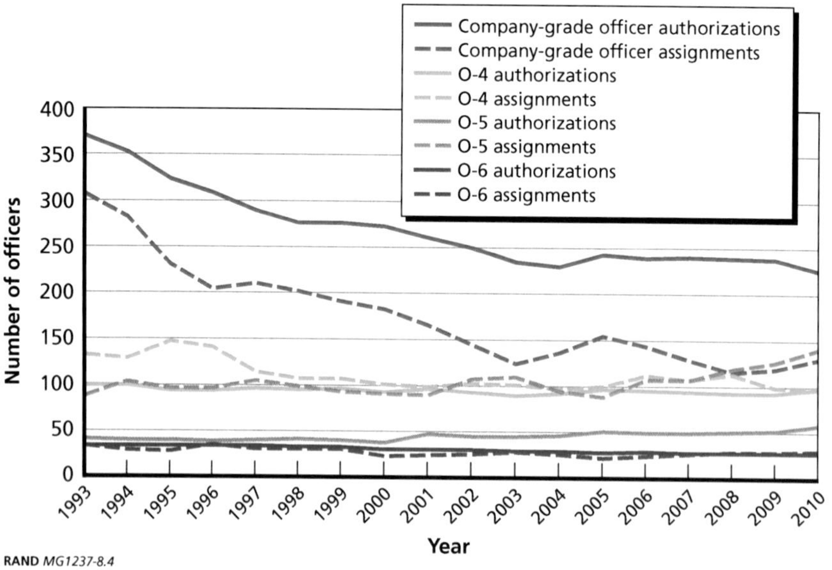

RAND *MG1237-8.4*

cers will then complete their payback tour after their doctorate, when they are field-grade officers. To the extent that USAFA prefers that its military faculty hold doctorates, these officers will most certainly be field grade. In other cases, assignment priorities make it less likely that officers will be available to teach at USAFA. Finally, as described in Chapter Seven, assignment teams are often wary of giving up their best people to teach at USAFA for fear that they will then be sponsored for a doctorate and follow-on tour, removing them from the career field and making them unavailable to fill operational billets for an extended period.

Summary

In conclusion, we found that faculty tours at USAFA do not always fit designated career paths and can result in missed opportunities for operational and command experience compared to non-faculty peers. This is particularly the case when officers obtain both a master's degree and a doctorate and complete two payback teaching tours at USAFA. Consistent with this finding, promotion analyses indicate that officers who taught at USAFA as company-grade officers only experienced less negative impact on their career advancement compared with officers who taught at USAFA as field-grade officers only or as both company-grade and field-grade officers. Thus, our findings suggest that sending officers to teach at USAFA early in their careers is important for officer career development. This is also the best option for producing a second graduating class with the potential to advance to higher ranks as a result of greater command opportunities.

However, there is currently a misalignment between manpower authorizations and assignments, with company-grade officers understaffed at USAFA. Company-grade officers are not understaffed across the Air Force, though. Rather, challenges related to the timing of degrees, career paths, and staffing practices focused on finding officers with doctorates contribute to the misalignment at USAFA. This suggests that, to avoid a negative impact on officer career development, there will need to be coordination in changing staffing practices to ensure that company-grade officer authorizations can be filled.

CHAPTER NINE

Conclusion and Policy Recommendations

Finding the best composition of military and civilian faculty to achieve USAFA's mission has been an issue since USAFA's founding. It is also very difficult for USAFA to find military officers with the appropriate advanced academic degrees to meet its needs, creating further challenges in maintaining a qualified faculty. Therefore, the goal of this research was to examine how general shifts in the current composition of military and civilian faculty would affect factors that are important to achieving USAFA's mission and the broader Air Force. We identified five factors that we considered critical to examine:

1. cadets' officership development
2. cadets' academic development
3. cost
4. staffing challenges
5. officer career development.

In this chapter, we provide an overview of our key findings for each of these factors.

Cadets' Officership Development

The qualitative findings from our interviews with USAFA senior leaders and faculty focus groups indicate that military faculty members play a key role in cadets' officership development. Specifically, military faculty members serve as role models, bring real operational experience to the classroom, and provide career advice. Results from a cadet survey further support this distinction in faculty roles. Although differences were often small, compared with civilian faculty, cadets rated military faculty members as having a greater influence on several aspects of their officer development. It is important to note, however, that cadets rated the military training staff (AOCs and AMTs) as having an equal or greater influence on aspects of their officership development compared with academic military faculty members.

Cadets' Academic Development

We were not able to find conclusive evidence of statistically significant differences in teaching effectiveness across faculty types. Additionally, the cadet survey results indicate only minimal differences in how cadets perceive the influence of faculty groups on their intellectual skill development and the extent to which different faculty groups bring greater academic depth of knowledge to the classroom. However, the qualitative findings from our interviews with USAFA senior leaders and faculty focus groups indicate that civilian faculty members serve a key academic function at USAFA that military faculty members are not able to fill in the same way. USAFA senior leaders and faculty identified civilians as providing continuity and stability, academic rigor and teaching expertise, connections with broader academia and the research community, and perspectives that differ from those brought by military personnel. The majority of civilian faculty members also hold doctorates, and, compared with military faculty, they have more teaching experience and tend to hold higher academic ranks.

Cost

In our analysis of the relative cost of employing a military officer or a civilian as a faculty member, we found that the average annual cost of employing a civilian is considerably lower than that of employing a military officer as a faculty member. After factoring in the amortized cost of obtaining an Air Force–sponsored master's degree, the average annual cost of a military faculty member can be twice that of a civilian faculty member; the cost differential is even greater for military faculty with an Air Force–sponsored doctorate.

Staffing Challenges

USAFA currently faces difficulties in filling military faculty positions because of the limited number of officers with the required advanced academic degrees, staff allocation plans for the broader Air Force that prioritize other billets, misalignment with career paths, and officer deployments. Further, due to budget limitations, funding for temporary faculty to fill these empty positions is also being reduced.

Officer Career Development

Finally, we examined the impact of USAFA instructor duty on the professional development of officers who are sent to teach. Our research found that faculty tours at USAFA do not always fit designated career paths and result in missed opportunities for operational and command experiences compared with non-faculty military peers. Consistent with this finding, promotion analyses indicated that those who taught at USAFA only as company-grade officers had better overall advancement rates to higher pay grades than officers who taught at USAFA as field-grade officers only or officers who taught as both company-grade and field-grade officers. Thus, our findings suggest that sending officers to teach at USAFA early in their careers is important for officer career development. This is also the best approach for producing what USAFA terms a "second graduating class" that has the potential to advance to higher ranks. Specifically, if we accept USAFA's assertion that instructor duty is beneficial for officer development, such a change will allow these officers to have this opportunity earlier and to provide a benefit to the broader Air Force for a longer period. This type of military faculty model is also more consistent with that of USMA, which fills the majority of its military faculty billets with company-grade officers.

However, company-grade officers are currently understaffed at USAFA due to timing of obtaining advanced degrees and assignment prioritizations. Company-grade officers are not understaffed across the Air Force, however. Instead, challenges regarding the timing of degrees, career paths, and staffing practices focused on finding officers with doctorates contribute to the misalignment at USAFA.

Impact of Five Potential Staffing Options

In Table 9.1, we list five potential staffing options focused on general shifts in the percentage of authorized military and civilian faculty posi-

Table 9.1
Impact of Staffing Options on Key Factors

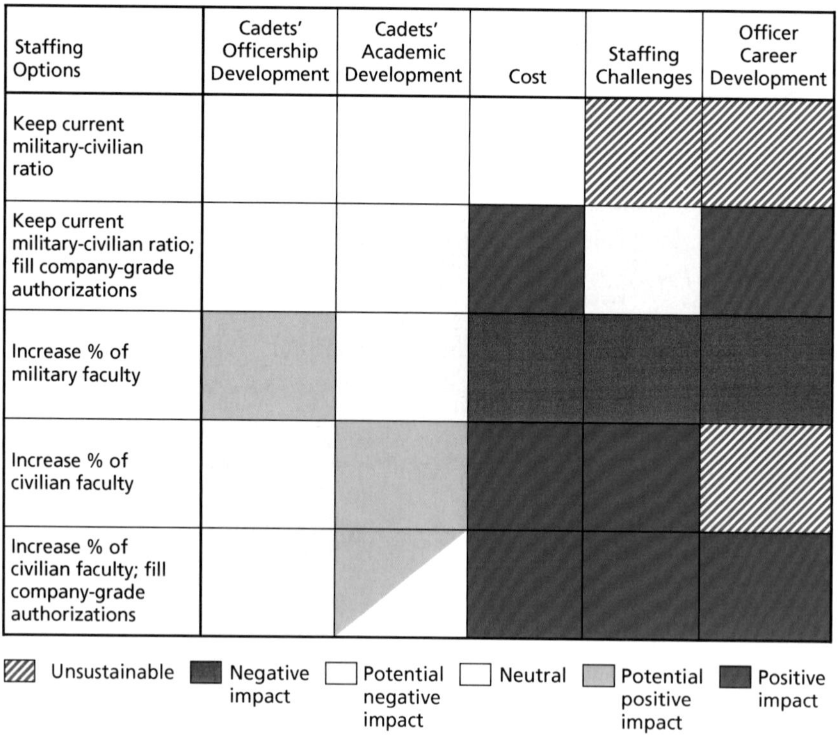

tions and addressing the current misalignment in manpower authorizations and assignments by filling current company-grade authorizations. Based on the study findings, we examined the impact that each of these shifts would have on the five factors examined in this research, compared with maintaining the current faculty authorizations.

Option 1 is to keep the current authorized percentages of military and civilian faculty, which would have a neutral impact across all factors. However, as highlighted in Table 9.1, maintaining current authorizations is likely not sustainable and would be undesirable for USAFA; it would perpetuate the challenges USAFA currently faces in finding military officers with the appropriate advanced academic degrees and the staffing practices that negatively affect officer career development.

Option 2 is to, again, keep the current authorized percentages of military and civilian faculty, but focus on fixing current staffing practices to fill the current authorizations for company-grade officers. Again, this option should have a neutral impact on cadets' officership development because there would be no change in the representation of military faculty. This option would have a positive impact on officer career development and also reduce costs, since company-grade officers are less expensive than higher-ranking officers. However, there is a potential negative impact on cadets' academic development if this shift results in a greater number of military faculty members coming to USAFA with only master's degrees and no prior teaching experience. This shift could be particularly detrimental to USAFA's ability to meet academic accreditation standards. In addition, there may be some initial challenges in shifting current staffing practices to ensure that company-grade officers obtain their degrees in time to teach and are available for faculty duty. Finally, with no shift in the total number of military faculty authorizations, general challenges in finding officers to teach are also likely to remain.

Option 3 is to increase the authorized percentage of military faculty members at USAFA. This option would have a negative impact across several factors. Although there is a potential positive impact on cadets' officership development, there is a potential negative impact on academic development. An increase in the representation of military faculty members would result in fewer civilian faculty members and, thus, likely fewer faculty members with the necessary teaching experience, doctorates, and ties to academia and the research community to meet accreditation standards. The lower representation of civilians also means that fewer faculty members in each department would be able to provide continuity and stability in the academic programs, as well as the requisite teaching expertise and mentoring to new rotating officers. Trying to fill more officer positions would also negatively affect cost. On average, employing a military officer is more costly than employing a civilian; it is even higher when one factors in the cost for an Air Force–sponsored advanced academic degree. Current staffing challenges in finding officers with the appropriate advanced academic degrees would also be exacerbated. Finally, this option also does not address the current understaffing of company-grade officers at USAFA, and increasing military representation would only result in a greater number of officers being removed from their primary career fields to fulfill a teaching tour. Therefore, this option would also have a negative impact on officer career development.

Option 4 is to increase the authorized percentage of civilian faculty at USAFA. This option would have a positive impact across many of the factors, including cadets' academic development, cost, and staffing. We were not able to find conclusive results when examining differences in the teaching effectiveness of military and civilian faculty. However, our qualitative data indicate that civilians play an overall important academic role at USAFA beyond just classroom instruction. Assuming that the Academy hires civilians of a high academic caliber, a greater number of civilians would be available to provide stability and continuity in academic programs, reenforce ties to broader academia, and facilitate research opportunities for cadets. A greater number of faculty members would also have doctorates and the domain expertise that comes with the degree. Therefore, increasing civilian representation would have a potentially positive impact on overall academics at USAFA. Additionally, on average, employing a civilian as a faculty member is less costly than employing a military officer. Staffing challenges should also lessen as fewer military officers are required for faculty tours. There is a potential negative impact on cadets' officership development, however. Finally, although this option would result in fewer military officers in total, it does not explicitly address issues with officer career development created by the current understaffing of company-grade officers at USAFA (this is addressed in option 5). Therefore, while the impact on officer career development remains neutral, we reiterate the unsustainability of this approach and the continuing negative impact on officer career development, as coded in Table 9.1.

Option 5 is to increase the authorized percentage of civilian faculty at USAFA and to focus on fixing current staffing practices to fill the current authorizations for company-grade officers. Given the increase in civilian representation, there would still be a potential negative impact on cadets' officership development because there would be fewer military faculty members. However, as described earlier, increased civilian representation would have a potentially positive impact on cadets' academic development and a clear positive impact on cost. The potential positive impact on academics could ultimately be washed out, though, if filling company-grade authorizations results in a greater number of military faculty with only master's degrees and no prior teaching experience. Therefore, USAFA would need to ensure that there is a proper balance to maintain the potential positive academic impact brought by an increase in civilian faculty. Additionally, although there could be initial challenges in changing staffing practices to fill company-grade authorizations, we believe that the reduction in the number of military faculty needed to teach at USAFA in light of the increased civilian representation under this option would result in an overall positive impact and help reduce staffing challenges. Finally, this option would have a positive impact on officer career development.

Thus, as Table 9.1 shows, increasing civilian representation would have a positive impact across many factors, and working to fill current company-grade authorizations would help facilitate officer career development. It is important to note, however, that the ultimate impact of any of these options on each of these factors depends on the degree of the change.

Recommendations

Based on the above analysis, we developed the following four recommendations. It is important to note that we do not believe there is a silver-bullet ratio of military to civilian faculty. We also treated all factors equally in developing our recommendations. The Air Force will ultimately need to make strategic decisions regarding which factors are the highest priorities while at the same time acknowledging the consequences that may result for the other factors.

Recommendation 1: A shift toward greater civilian representation is advisable, unless its potential negative impact on building cadet officership outweighs the other factors. Increasing the authorized percentage of civilian faculty would have the most positive impact across factors. Despite the potential negative impact on cadets' officership development, cost and staffing challenges would be reduced, and there is a potential positive impact on academics, assuming that high-quality civilians are hired. As stated previously, our analysis did not result in any silver bullet ratio of military and civilian faculty. However, if the Air Force chooses to shift toward greater civilian representation, one option is a gradual increase in civilian representation toward roughly 40 percent of the authorized positions, which would work to formalize current operating conditions at USAFA. Although the authorized mix of faculty at USAFA is 71 percent military and 29 percent civilian, actual civilian representation when accounting for military faculty shortages and temporary instructors was as high as 37 percent in spring 2011, when this research was completed. Based on the total number of faculty authorizations at the time of this research (570 positions), this would result in a shift of roughly 64 authorized faculty positions to civilian. In our focus groups and interviews, many faculty members and division/department heads described the current faculty mix as working well. Presumably, then, a shift toward formalizing this mix should have a minimal negative impact on USAFA, particularly in terms of officership development. If such a shift were to occur gradually over the next five years, it would result in a rough estimated cumulative savings of more than $21 million.[1] We also recommend that this be a gradual shift, allowing for the monitoring of potential negative effects that may not have been identified through the current research.

Recommendation 2: The mix of military and civilian faculty should vary across departments, with military representation concentrated in academic disciplines that are needed elsewhere in the Air Force. As discussed in Chapter Seven, finding military faculty with the appropriate advanced academic degrees to teach in academic departments that are not directly aligned with an Air Force specialty or highly utilized in the broader Air Force is very challenging. Therefore, we do not recommend a one-size-fits-all ratio across departments. Instead, departments should be allowed to vary in their mix of military and civilian faculty. This is also consistent with our findings from interviews with USAFA senior leaders, who indicated that they did not necessarily believe that there was one correct mix across academic departments. The intent is not necessarily for any departments to become entirely civilian; rather, departments should strategically decide how best to staff their faculty. This approach would also help provide better payback for the costs of Air Force–sponsored advanced academic degrees, since the Air Force could concentrate on sponsoring degrees in disciplines that can be utilized elsewhere in the Air Force.

---

[1] As an estimate of the savings that could be realized, we modeled a reduction of O-4 and O-5 faculty distributed in the same ratio as the current faculty with respect to military rank and academic rank. Because military personnel serve at USAFA for an average of only three years, they do not have the same opportunity to obtain academic rank as their civilian faculty counterparts. To ensure high-quality academic qualifications across the faculty, for this savings scenario, we substituted civilian faculty for military faculty at the next higher academic rank. For example, if a military major/O-4 assistant professor position were to be converted, the new civilian position would be at the associate professor level. We could assume that all military faculty members who are to be replaced by civilians are direct hires and that there were no costs incurred for their advanced academic degrees. This assumption serves as a floor (minimum) for the possible savings in this scenario—$7.38 million over the five-year period. If, instead, the converted military faculty positions had been filled by faculty who received Air Force–sponsored degrees, the savings would be much greater. Our sample scenario projected an estimated $1.37 million in savings in year 1 with the conversion of 13 military faculty positions. Savings in year 5, after the conversion of 64 positions, would grow to $6.84 million, resulting in a cumulative savings of over $21 million.

Recommendation 3: Align military faculty assignments with manpower grade authorizations by filling current authorizations for company-grade officers. This recommendation, along with the recommendation to increase the percentage of authorized civilian faculty members, represents option 5 in Table 9.1. Our research indicates that those who taught at USAFA only as company-grade officers had better overall advancement rates to higher pay grades than officers who taught at USAFA as field-grade officers only or officers who taught as both company-grade and field-grade officers. Thus, it is important to send officers to teach at USAFA early in their careers, when USAFA instructor duty will not hinder future advancement opportunities. This would also be the best approach for producing what USAFA terms a "second graduating class" that will be able to advance to higher ranks. However, current staffing practices result in overstaffing of field-grade and understaffing of company-grade officers at USAFA. Therefore, working to fill current authorizations for company-grade officers would help address this misalignment and ensure that more officers' career advancement potential will not be hindered by instructor duty at USAFA.

Of course, there may be some initial challenges to achieving this realignment. Specifically, there will need to be considerable coordination and trust between AFPC and USAFA so that instructor duty becomes a valuable developmental experience and not a risk that the officer will be taken away from his or her career field. Additionally, the Air Force will have to work to ensure that officers are obtaining their advanced academic degrees early enough to ensure that they have the opportunity to fulfill instructor duty when they are junior officers.

Finally, it should be noted that this recommendation focuses only on aligning current assignments with manpower grade authorizations. Field-grade officers play an important role at USAFA, and we are not recommending that the military faculty be composed of only company-grade officers. Field-grade officers are important in acting as more senior and experienced role models to cadets and serving in key leadership and governance positions. Furthermore, it is also important to maintain a high-quality pool of field-grade officers from which to draw USAFA faculty with the designation of Permanent Professor.

Recommendation 4: The Air Force should monitor and assess the impact of any changes to the current military and civilian faculty mix on USAFA's ability to fulfill its mission. As USAFA implements any changes to the composition of its faculty, it will be important to monitor any potentially negative effects on the factors examined as part of this research and on the overall ability of USAFA to fulfill its mission. For example, USAFA has outlined distinct leadership competencies that cadets are expected to develop each year as part of the PITO model. In addition to these leadership competencies, USAFA has outlined specific responsibility, skill, and knowledge outcomes that all cadets are expected to achieve upon graduation.[2] Although academic faculty may not be expected to directly facilitate each of these designated outcomes, USAFA should ensure that it has reliable and valid measures for each of these outcomes and can examine whether there are significant changes in these areas as changes are made to the faculty composition.

Additionally, in conducting this study, we tried to focus on criteria that are important to the mission of USAFA and the broader Air force. However, there is potential for unforeseen impact, either positive or negative, in areas not identified as part of this study. Therefore, academic department heads will want to monitor how shifts in the faculty composition affect overall department functioning and the fulfillment of faculty duties.

Conclusion

We do not believe that there is a silver-bullet ratio or mix of military and civilian faculty at USAFA. Ultimately, the weight given to each factor in this analysis is a strategic decision that must be made by Air Force leaders. Further, although we included the factors that we identified as most critical to the mission of USAFA and the broader Air Force, other factors may become more or less important in the future. For example, with fewer deployments, some challenges in find-

---

[2] For more information see HQ USAFA Pamphlet 36-3527, 2008.

ing military faculty may lessen. However, holding these factors equal, we believe that a shift in the faculty toward greater civilian representation in the authorized positions will not be harmful to USAFA but will instead have the most positive impact. We also believe that working to better fill current authorizations for company-grade officers will have positive benefits for the broader Air Force.

In terms of next steps, the Air Force leadership will need to critically examine how to best implement any shifts in the faculty composition. This is not a change that can take place overnight; it must happen gradually as new faculty positions open. There must also be considerable coordination between USAFA and the personnel responsible for military faculty assignments and those in charge of managing the advanced academic degree process to ensure that officers obtain their degrees early enough to teach as company-grade officers. It will also be important to understand the different departmental duties performed by different faculty groups and to ensure that manpower is sufficient to continue these duties as the faculty composition shifts. However, overall, we believe that staffing challenges should improve with increased civilian representation, particularly by concentrating civilians in academic departments that have the most challenges in finding military officers with the appropriate advanced academic degrees. Taken together, we believe the above recommendations will result in a USAFA faculty that is better able to help the Academy fulfill its mission and is more sustainable into the future.

APPENDIX A

Historical Background

This appendix provides a brief history of the seminal events surrounding the issue of faculty composition at the U.S. service academies and USAFA in particular.

The Early Years: The Stearns-Eisenhower Report

While 1954 marked the official establishment of USAFA, the issue of faculty composition at the Academy actually predates that event. In 1949, Secretary of Defense Louis Johnson commissioned the Service Academy Board to recommend "the manner in which officer candidates should receive their basic education for a career in the services."[1] After the study, the board released the *Stearns-Eisenhower Report*, which, in addition to recommending the establishment of the Air Force Academy, examined many elements of the organizational structure and operation of the already existing USMA and USNA.

In profiling the faculty systems of the existing service academies, the report focused on faculty composition and included a recommendation for the future faculty composition of USAFA. All told, five of its nine main recommendations directly related to improving faculty composition:

[1] U.S. Department of Defense, *Stearns-Eisenhower Report: A Report and Recommendation to the Secretary of Defense by the Service Academy Board*, January 1950, p. 1.

1. That it be made possible for the heads of the Departments at all the Academies to have Permanent Appointments

2. That the method of appointing civilian instructors and professors now authorized by law for the Naval Academy be made available to the other two services. The appointment of these civilian faculty members should not be restricted by civil service procedures.

3. That the authority to commission permanent professors from civilian life with appropriate military rank be extended to all the services.

4. That the practice of allowing the Superintendents a high priority in choosing the members of the regular services as faculty members be continued.

5. That exchange professorships with civilian institutions be developed with appropriate provision for expenses that may be incurred, and that provision be made for sabbatical or other leave with pay for the purposes of the study.[2]

In examining the faculty at USMA, which was composed largely of military officers serving three-year tours of duty, the Service Academy Board highlighted as weaknesses the high rate of faculty turnover and lack of faculty with advanced degrees or training in certain academic fields. To remedy these weaknesses, the board recommended that mechanisms be enacted to increase the proportion of permanent, non-rotational faculty members to 25 percent in science and engineering fields and more in the humanities and social sciences. To remedy the lack of faculty members with advanced degrees or training, the board recommended that USMA employ individuals who possessed such qualifications, and "if necessary, [that] these men should be commissioned to place them on the basis of staff equality with other members of the faculty."[3]

---

[2] DoD, 1950, p. 14.

[3] DoD, 1950, p. 48.

The Service Academy Board noted that, unlike USMA, USNA had a large population of civilian faculty members. However, it also stressed the high rate of rotation among naval officers as an issue. The *Stearns-Eisenhower Report* provided further guidance related to USNA faculty issues, recommending that it employ visiting professors, increase faculty participation in professional academic societies, implement sabbatical leave for advanced study, and establish new promotion and salary policies to ensure that military officers' career paths were not inadvertently hindered by serving in academic faculty positions.

Other sections of the *Stearns-Eisenhower Report* discussed additional issues related to faculty composition. A separate study on teaching and testing methods in the service academies provided additional guidance on selecting and improving their faculty. Recommendations included provisions for civilian faculty members to receive tenure and retirement annuities, revisions of the promotion system to prevent faculty duty from becoming a "dead-end" assignment, and increases in the number of professionally prepared civilian instructors in DoD by 50 percent, with the goal of integrating them into the overall faculties of the academies.[4]

A separate examination of language and area studies at the academies resulted in the recommendation that the USNA practice of "engaging civilian instructors independent of Civil Service should be extended to other Academies."[5] The report further examined the trade-offs between military officers and civilian language faculty, citing continuity and uniformity of instruction as benefits of employing civilians and stating that lengthy tours in language instruction detract from a military officer's career progression. Panelists concluded that a core group of career civilian faculty complemented by rotational military faculty would be beneficial to enhanced instruction, but "other things being equal, officer instructors are preferable in a military academy."[6]

---

4 DoD, 1950, p. 69.

5 DoD, 1950, p. 64.

6 DoD, 1950, p. 65.

When USAFA officially began operating in 1954, many functional areas and facets of cadet life were modeled after USMA,[7] including the faculty composition, which was almost completely military. In stark contrast, at the time of USAFA's inception, USNA employed a roughly equal proportion of military and civilian academic faculty members; to this day, USNA continues to aim for this 50/50 ratio of military and civilian faculty.[8] Given the historical similarities in the faculty composition between USAFA and USMA, research and analysis on this issue generally contrast the high percentage of military faculty at USMA and USAFA with the evenly divided academic faculty of USNA. The similarities between the historical faculty composition at USMA and USAFA make research specific to faculty composition issues at one institution relevant to the other.

Continuing Debate Over Issues of Faculty Composition in the 1960s and 1970s

Following the formation of USAFA in 1954, issues surrounding the faculty composition continued into the 1960s and 1970s. Furthermore, while the multiple Stearns-Eisenhower faculty composition recommendations were all aligned with the goal of providing the best method of developing officer candidates for service as officers in the U.S. armed forces, later discussions pertaining to USAFA's faculty composition included other factors—such as cost—as a means of evaluating the ideal military-civilian mix.

A push for greater civilian faculty representation continued throughout the 1960s and 1970s. For example, in 1973, Deputy Secretary of Defense William P. Clements Jr. formed the Committee on Excellence in Education to review educational programs in DoD. This

---

[7] John P. Lovell, *Neither Athens Nor Sparta? The American Service Academies in Transition*, Bloomington, Ind.: Indiana University Press, 1979.

[8] Office of the Assistant Secretary of Defense for Force Management and Personnel, *A Blend of Excellence: Military-Civilian Faculty Mix at the Service Academies*, Washington, D.C., 1993.

committee—composed of the Secretaries of the Army, Navy, and Air Force, as well as the Assistant Secretary of Defense for Manpower and Reserve Affairs—examined many facets of the service academies, including the issue of military-civilian faculty mix.[9] Releasing a summary of its findings in April 1975, the committee did not specify an ideal ratio of military to civilian faculty members, but it concluded that USAFA, along with USMA, should slightly increase its numbers of civilian faculty, while USNA should increase its utilization of military faculty so that there would be more junior military faculty bringing their operational experiences into the classroom.

More specifically, the committee recommended that USAFA and USMA analyze the advantage of adding civilian faculty members to bring the level to between 5 and 10 percent by 1980. As for USNA, the committee suggested increasing the level of military faculty from 50 percent to 65 percent by 1980 and eventually to a level that reflected the proportion of military faculty at USAFA and USMA.[10] As implied in its recommendations concerning military-civilian faculty composition, the committee believed that "military officers were to be preferred to civilians as role models in constituting the faculties of the academies."[11]

However, simultaneous studies of service academy operations yielded different implications for faculty composition. A 1975 U.S. General Accounting Office (GAO) study of service academy financial operations concluded that the high percentage of military faculty at USAFA and USMA yielded much higher costs than the roughly equal mix of military and civilian faculty at USNA.[12] At the same time, however, a separate 1975 GAO report cited USNA's need to upgrade its

---

9 Lovell, 1979.

10 Elmer B. Staats, Comptroller General of the United States, Education: Federal Service Academies, statement before the Subcommittee on Legislation and National Security, Committee on Government Operations Concerning the Federal Service Academies, U.S. House of Representatives, Washington, D.C., March 17, 1976.

11 Lovell, 1979, p. 223.

12 Comptroller General of the United States, *Financial Operations of the Five Service Academies*, Washington, D.C.: U.S. General Accounting Office, FPCD-75-117, February 1975a.

academic faculty, arguing that 25 percent did not possess advanced academic degrees.[13] In 1975, civilians composed only 1 percent of the USAFA faculty, and the GAO highlighted in that same report how the much larger percentage of military faculty creates a highly rotational, inexperienced faculty. The report mentioned that although USAFA operated a brief introductory training program for new military faculty members, the Academy's leadership assumed that incoming faculty's academic degrees, excellent Air Force performance records, and past experiences in instructing operational military skill or field training would yield competent instructors. The GAO was "not convinced . . . that these experiences, as well as the instructor training programs, adequately prepare new faculty members."[14] In this regard, it agreed with the recommendation of the earlier Committee on Excellence in Education that USMA and USAFA needed to investigate the feasibility of increasing their civilian faculty presence to between 5 and 10 percent as a way of increasing the overall faculty experience level.

However, these same GAO reports challenged the committee's conclusion that military faculty members serve as role models of military service. In 1976 congressional testimony, the U.S. Comptroller General discussed the services' major argument that military faculty motivate cadets and midshipmen to pursue careers in military service. A survey administered to service academy cadets and midshipmen, dropouts, and graduates asked these individuals about the number of courses in which the "instructor motivated me toward a career in the service," and how likely they were "to make the military or maritime industry your career." Responses to the first question revealed that a significantly higher percentage of courses motivated career military service at USAFA and USMA—which were heavy on military faculty—compared with USNA. While this correlation seemed to indicate the ability of a military faculty member to motivate career military service, the finding was undercut by the fact that more than 50 percent

---

[13] Comptroller General of the United States, *Academic and Military Programs of the Five Service Academies*, Washington, D.C.: U.S. General Accounting Office, FPCD-76-8, October 1975b.

[14] Comptroller General of the United States, 1975b, p. 9.

of USAFA and USMA graduates indicated that fewer than half of their courses motivated them toward career military service. In addition, GAO analysis of responses to the second survey question indicated that first-year (freshman) cadets and midshipmen possessed greater motivation for a military career than upper-class cadets and midshipmen, possibly indicating that the service academy experience actually *decreases* motivation for career military service. Overall, the Comptroller General stated that factors external to the service academies, notably active-duty experiences, extended service obligations as a result of training, and external societal and economic conditions were more influential in terms of individual career military service decisions.[15]

Continuing Debate Over Faculty Composition in the 1990s

Despite the recommendations of various stakeholders, USAFA maintained an almost entirely military faculty throughout the 1970s and 1980s. As of 1990, civilians accounted for only 2–3 percent of its faculty, and a large contingent of these civilians were visiting professors from other institutions.[16] USAFA justified its heavy focus on military faculty by citing several perceived advantages: Military officers serve as role models, they motivate career military service in cadets, they connect course themes to operational military issues, they provide assistance in military training, they gain valuable teaching experience, and they understand the importance of teaching over research and publications.[17]

Although USAFA's largely military faculty may have yielded such benefits, various bodies voiced concern about the academic creden-

---

[15] Staats, 1976.

[16] Paul L. Jones, director, Manpower Issues, National Security, and International Affairs Division, U.S. General Accounting Office, *Review of the Cost and Operations of DoD's Service Academies*, statement before the Subcommittee on Manpower and Personnel, Committee on Armed Services, U.S. Senate, Washington, D.C.: U.S. General Accounting Office, GAO/T-NSIAD-90-28, April 4, 1990.

[17] Jones, 1990.

tials of the USAFA faculty during the 1990s. For example, a July 1991 GAO report investigated many aspects of DoD service academy operations and expressed concerns over recent accreditation reports. At the time, only 38 percent of USAFA faculty had doctorates, and USAFA's 1989 accreditation review, conducted by the North Central Association of Colleges and Schools, stated that "the intellectual vitality and depth of the faculty as a whole are adversely affected by the relative lack of PhDs among the faculty."[18] Furthermore, while the accreditation report praised the USAFA faculty's "strong esprit de corps" and dedication to the Academy's goals, it questioned the ability of USAFA's highly rotational faculty to stay "abreast of the current scholarship and developments" in their fields of instruction.[19] USAFA visiting professors faulted the high faculty turnover rate for leading to high levels of inexperience among the faculty and for impeding the scholarly environment at USAFA.

DoD only partially concurred with the findings of the GAO's inquiry into service academy academic and faculty composition; it also characterized the accreditation body's concerns about the low percentage of qualified faculty and high faculty turnover as not representative of the entire mass of accreditation body findings.[20] DoD determined that such criticism was misguided because of differences between the research agendas and teaching structures at civilian institutions and those at the service academies made the two incomparable. Congressional testimony by Lt Gen Charles R. Hamm, then superintendent of USAFA, also underscored the role of military faculty as role models and criticized comparing USAFA doctoral-level faculty to peers at research-oriented civilian institutions. According to General Hamm, making such a comparison was inappropriate because doctoral-level faculty at civilian institutions focused primarily on research and publishing, leaving actual classroom instruction to graduate assistants, many of whom

---

[18] Jones, 1990, p. 7.

[19] U.S. General Accounting Office, *DoD Service Academies: Improved Cost and Performance Monitoring Needed*, Washington, D.C., GAO-NSIAD-91-79, July 1991, p. 25.

[20] GAO, 1991.

held only undergraduate degrees. According to General Hamm, the only staff who taught at USAFA had earned at least a master's degree.[21]

Although the GAO, academic accreditation bodies, and congressional leaders supported an increase in USAFA civilian faculty to improve the overall quality of the academic program, USAFA and USMA leadership continued to oppose the increased presence of civilians on the academic faculty. Nevertheless, the National Defense Authorization Bill for Fiscal Year 1993 directed the Secretary of Defense "to submit legislation . . . to conform faculty staffing at the USMA and the USAFA to the faculty staffing at the USNA (50/50 military/civilian mix)."[22] USMA leadership was initially displeased with this and other components of the legislation. As a result, a series of negotiations between different DoD and congressional stakeholders occurred, and an amendment was added to the legislation that directed the secretaries of the Army and Air Force to "employ as many civilians as professors, instructors, and lecturers at the Academy as the Secretary considers necessary" and report their planned changes by April 1993.[23] Thus, a compromise was reached wherein the respective service secretaries could decide on the appropriate percentage of civilian faculty at USMA and USAFA.

In April 1993, the Office of the Assistant Secretary of Defense for Force Management and Personnel released a report titled *A Blend of Excellence: Military-Civilian Faculty Mix at the Service Academies*, which contained a plan for USAFA and USMA to increase their cohort of civilian faculty while simultaneously reducing their military faculty. The report also defined the distinctive roles of military and civilian faculty; while arguing that the two types of faculty should have a common ground of disciplinary competency, it stated that military faculty should also demonstrate tenets of officership, while civilians

---

[21] Jones, 1990.

[22] House Resolution 5006, National Defense Authorization Act for Fiscal Year 1993, 102nd Congress, 1992. See also Rick Maze, "Bill Would Cut Status, Officer Staff at Academies," *Air Force Times*, Vol. 53, No. 11, October 19, 1992, p. 24.

[23] House Resolution 5006, Sec 523, Composition of Faculties at United States Military Academy and Air Force Academy, 1992.

should "be adept at educational innovation, and be abreast of educational advances."[24] Although the report delineates the roles of civilian and military faculty, it concludes that such faculty roles are not mutually exclusive and that "the faculties can act in unity but not identically—a blend of excellence."[25] To increase the proportion of USAFA civilian faculty, it outlines a plan for USAFA to hire civilian candidates with earned doctorates to increase the overall percentage of the civilian faculty to 26 percent by the year 2000. The report further directs that a large portion of initial civilian hires be from the younger associate professor ranks so that these faculty will remain and develop at USAFA for some time before retirement. It also stresses that the total percentage of USAFA faculty with doctorates should increase from 43 percent (the level in 1992) to 54 percent by the year 2000. With these projected changes, the report states, "faculty costs should not increase under the Department's proposal," because the anticipated projected salaries of the civilian faculty will range below the salaries provided to military faculty.[26]

The Larson Report

Following the directives put forth by Congress in 1993 and the resultant plan presented in *A Blend of Excellence*, USAFA gradually assimilated greater numbers of civilians onto its academic faculty. By 2004, civilians composed approximately 25 percent of the authorized academic faculty at USAFA.[27] In that same year, Congress commissioned a study of USAFA's faculty composition, commonly referred to as the Larson Report. The study concluded that the current faculty mix and

---

[24] Office of the Assistant Secretary of Defense for Force Management and Personnel, 1993, p. 2.

[25] Office of the Assistant Secretary of Defense for Force Management and Personnel, 1993, p. 2.

[26] Office of the Assistant Secretary of Defense for Force Management and Personnel, 1993, p. 4.

[27] Larson, 2004.

system had "evolved due to external factors and pressures rather than through a careful strategic analysis and evaluation of what the balance in the faculty system should be."[28] The Larson Report further criticized USAFA for failing to embrace the spirit and intent of congressional directives by employing retired military personnel in 30 percent of its civilian faculty positions. Admiral Larson, who led the committee, praised USMA for employing pure academicians in its civilian faculty cohort, in contrast to USAFA. The report also highlighted the issue of USAFA's increasingly senior civilian faculty being likely to continue to exert pressure on USAFA leadership for a tenure system, a greater leadership role, and increased involvement in overarching curriculum development.

Based on these findings, the Larson Report recommended that USAFA conduct a comprehensive self-study of all faculty elements, primarily hire pure academicians from civilian higher education, and strategically assess the voiced concerns of its civilian faculty. The report also mentioned recent problems related to the rotational military faculty, such as smaller volunteer numbers for faculty duty, overall lower personnel quality, and the small presence of rated officers in faculty positions. The report recommended that the Air Force give stronger support to the recruitment and retention of these personnel and stress the value of faculty service to career field advancement.

In response to the Larson Report, USAFA argued that accreditation results, graduate performance, and consultation with other DoD service academies confirmed that the 2004 USAFA faculty composition, with 75 percent military and 25 percent civilian faculty, would continue to meet Air Force and national needs.[29] It further contended that increasing the civilian presence beyond this level would impede USAFA's ability to effectively develop and prepare Air Force officers in accordance with the mantra that "warriors best produce warriors."[30] More recent congressional testimony by USAFA leadership has also extolled the high qualifications and awards garnered by both mili-

[28] Larson, 2004, p. 6-2.

[29] Born, 2004.

[30] Born, 2004, p. 4.

tary and civilian faculty members, but it also acknowledges the many challenges USAFA faces in managing its faculty against competing Air Force needs. For example, in a July 2009 statement to the House Oversight and Investigations Subcommittee of the Committee on Armed Services, USAFA's Dean of Faculty concluded that "most of the [USAFA's] challenges lie in attracting and maintaining the right mix of military faculty and arise due to competition with the operational needs of the Air Force."[31] While USAFA civilian faculty attrite at a 2-percent annual rate, Air Force shortages in rated officers, scientists, and engineers make it difficult for USAFA to pull such individuals out of their normal career paths for further academic development and a follow-on teaching assignment. Deployments of faculty members create further difficulties.

Finally, the issue of prior-service personnel composing a significant percentage of the civilian faculty population has continued to be a concern. For example, a 2010 report from the House Subcommittee on Oversight and Investigation found that "USAFA has not done enough to hire pure civilian faculty."[32] USAFA has stated that the civilian hiring process tries not to "advantage military or disadvantage military, retired military."[33] However, it also argued that prior-service personnel provide a beneficial balance of military experience and advanced scholarship that is not possible with purely civilian faculty.

Summary

As this appendix illustrates, securing an appropriate mix of military and civilian faculty at USAFA is an issue rooted deeply in the history of the institution. It has similarly been an issue for the other service academies. These concerns have focused on various factors, including the lack of advanced degrees and high turnover rates of military members, the cost-effectiveness of employing military and civilian faculty

---

31 Born, 2009, p. 4.

32 U.S. House of Representatives, 2010, p. 127.

33 Born, 2009, p. 25.

members, and academic accreditation challenges. As discussed in the body of this report, many of these same concerns continue today and led to the inclusion of many of the factors we addressed in our analysis.

APPENDIX B

Interview and Focus Group Method and Analysis

This appendix presents more detailed information on the participants, protocols, and analysis of the qualitative data gathered through our interviews and focus groups.

USAFA Senior Leader Interviews

We conducted semistructured interviews with USAFA senior leaders and academic division heads (all active-duty or retired Air Force officers). We later conducted another set of interviews with ten USAFA faculty in key leadership positions under the Dean of Faculty. Each interview lasted approximately 45–60 minutes. Two RAND researchers conducted each interview, with one researcher leading the interview and the other taking verbatim notes. The interviews were also recorded so that any inconsistencies or gaps in the notes could be corrected later. The interview questions focused primarily on the following three broad topics:

1. the role of different faculty types in helping USAFA achieve its mission
2. the ideal military-civilian faculty mix
3. challenges to achieving the ideal military-civilian faculty mix.

Faculty Focus Groups

As a follow-up to these interviews, we conducted 12 focus groups with current USAFA faculty members. To ensure that faculty members would feel comfortable discussing the issue of the military-civilian faculty mix at USAFA and to enable comparisons in the responses of different faculty types, we stratified our sample of focus group participants by military and civilian status. We further separated civilian faculty by prior service experience and separated military faculty by academic rank (academic rank often reflects military rank, with officers in the grades of captain/O-3 and major/O-4 predominantly serving as instructors) and commissioning source. At the request of USAFA, we also held two open focus group sessions for any faculty members who did not receive a request to participate in one of the official focus groups but were interested in voicing their opinions. Data from these open sessions were analyzed separately to account for potential differences in those who chose to participate.

Based on the purposeful stratification of our focus groups, we randomly selected faculty members to email for voluntary participation, which resulted in six to nine participants in each focus group. We also emailed all 20 academic department heads to participate.[1] This resulted in a total of 80 participants across the groups. The majority of faculty members who declined to participate cited scheduling conflicts as the primary reason. The two open session focus groups were advertised to all faculty members who were not selected for participation in one of our formal focus groups. Overall, we spoke to a diverse group of faculty members, spanning the range of academic rank, department, number of years teaching at USAFA, and military background.

The focus groups lasted approximately 90 minutes. The discussions were recorded, with one research team member moderating the focus group and a second research team member taking notes. These notes were later revised based on the audio recording. Focus group questions focused on the following three broad topics:

---

[1] Some department heads also serve as the overall academic division head and had been previously interviewed as part of our senior leader interviews at USAFA. These department heads were not contacted again to participate in the focus groups.

1. perceptions of USAFA's mission
2. the role of different faculty types in helping USAFA achieve its mission
3. staffing challenges.

We allowed the discussions to deviate from these themes to some degree, as each group focused on different topics in the discussion. However, we did discuss these issues in all focus groups.

The primary goal of the focus groups was to explore how faculty members perceive their roles in helping USAFA achieve its mission and whether these perceptions differed by faculty type. We heard similar themes across all focus groups and no longer heard new information in the later sessions. Therefore, consistent with recommendations for qualitative research, the lack of new themes indicated that we had reached theoretical saturation and additional focus groups would not be necessary for our explorative purposes.

Qualitative Data Analysis

Following recommendations for qualitative data analysis in the research literature,[2] we employed an iterative, multiphase approach in analyzing both the interview and focus group data. First, we used an open coding method in which we went through the transcripts line by line and took notes on emerging themes that were relevant to the key research questions. In the second step of the analysis, we grouped these themes into more abstract categories to develop a coding scheme for the transcripts. Two research team members hand-coded each interview transcript; we ensured that we had sufficient inter-rater reliability by calculating Cohen's kappa. Given the larger number and length of the transcripts for the focus groups, two research team members coded an overlapping 10 percent of the transcripts at the start of the coding process; when

[2] See Juliet M. Corbin and Anselm L. Strauss, *Basics of Qualitative Research: Techniques and Procedures for Developing Grounded Theory*, 3rd ed., Thousand Oaks, Calif.: Sage Publications, 2008; Mathew B. Miles, and A. Michael Huberman, *Qualitative Data Analysis: An Expanded Sourcebook*, 2nd ed., Thousand Oaks, Calif.: Sage Publications, 1994.

sufficient inter-rater reliability was met, the remaining transcripts were coded by a single research team member. A second set of overlapping transcripts was also included to recheck the inter-rater reliability.

USAFA Senior Leader Interview Protocol

Introductions, Informed Consent

Thank you very much for meeting with us today. We are here to gather information for a study sponsored by the Office of the Assistant Secretary of the Air Force for Manpower and Reserve Affairs (SAF/MR) and the Office of the Deputy Chief of Staff for Manpower, Personnel, and Services (AF/A1). The primary objective of the study is to assess civilian and military faculty staffing at the Academy.

[Insert informed consent materials here.]

We would like to start with some general background information about you.

General Background

1. Please, describe your current position at the Academy.
2. Please, describe your responsibilities at the Academy.
3. How long have you served in this position?
4. Have you held other positions at the Academy?
   a. [If answer is YES]: What have those other positions been?
5. How long have you been with the Air Force?

Academy Mission

1. How would you describe the overall mission of the Academy?
   a. What is the mission of your specific mission element/academic division?
2. How do you go about achieving this mission?
3. What is the role of faculty members in achieving the mission?
   a. How do you define "faculty"?
   b. What are the different types of faculty (e.g., rank/positions)?

   c. Do different types of faculty serve different roles in achieving the Academy's mission (e.g., civilian vs. active-duty; instructors, assistant professors, associate professors, full professors, permanent professors)?
   d. Describe the responsibilities of different types of faculty.
4. Describe what you see as the importance of having civilian members as part of the faculty.
   a. What are the background experiences you look for in hiring civilian faculty?
      ◦ How many of the civilian faculty are retired military?
5. Describe what you see as the importance of having military members as part of the faculty.
   a. What are the background experiences you look for in selecting military faculty?
6. Do you utilize National Guard and reserve members to fill faculty positions?
   a. [If answer is YES]: Describe what you see as the importance of having Guard and reserve members as part of the faculty.

We would now like to gather information about the current mix of civilian and military faculty.

Mix of Civilian and Military Faculty

1. Describe the current mix or ratio of civilian and military faculty at the Academy.
   a. Describe the current mix or ratio of civilian and military faculty/staff in your academic division.
2. Is this particular mix or ratio a goal or standard that the Academy tries to maintain?
   a. Can you describe the reason for the particular ratio?
      ◦ Explicit policy, law, directive from senior leaders, etc.?
      ◦ Studies, reports?

3. How has the mix or ratio of civilian and military faculty at the Academy changed over the years?
   a. What are the reasons for the changes?
   b. How have those changes affected the culture of the Academy?
   c. How have those changes affected the ability of the Academy or your academic division to achieve its mission?
4. Describe what you think would be the ideal mix or ratio of civilian and military faculty members.
   a. Why this mix or ratio?
   b. What criteria are you using to develop your opinion of the ideal mix or ratio?
5. Describe any challenges you face in achieving this ideal mix or ratio?
   a. Do you have difficulty hiring civilians for open positions and, if so, why?
   b. Do you have difficulty finding military personnel for open positions and, if so, why?
6. How would changing the mix of civilian and military faculty affect the culture of the Academy?
   a. How much of a change would this have to be to have an effect?
7. How would changing the mix of civilian and military faculty affect the ability of your academic division to achieve its mission?

Closing Comments and Thanks

Thank you so much for meeting with us today. The information you provided is critical for our analysis. We will keep you updated on our progress.

USAFA Focus Group Protocol

Introductions, Informed Consent

Thank you very much for meeting with us today. We are here to gather information for a study sponsored by the Office of the Assistant Secretary of the Air Force for Manpower and Reserve Affairs (SAF/MR) and the Office of the Deputy Chief of Staff for Manpower, Personnel, and Services (AF/A1). The primary objective of the study is to assess civilian and military faculty staffing at the Academy.

[Insert informed consent materials here.]

We would like to start with some general background information about you.

General Background

1. Please, describe your current position at the Academy.
2. Please, describe your responsibilities at the Academy.
3. How long have you served in this position?
4. Have you held other positions at the Academy?
   a. [If answer is YES]: What have those other positions been?

Now we would like to ask you a few questions about the mission of the Academy and faculty roles.

Faculty Roles

1. How would you describe the overall mission of the Academy?
2. What is the role of the faculty members in achieving the mission?
   a. Do different types of faculty serve different roles in achieving the mission (e.g., civilian vs. active-duty; instructors,

assistant professors, associate professors, full professors, permanent professors)?

b. Describe responsibilities of different types of faculty.
c. Describe what you see as the importance of having civilian members as part of the faculty.
   - Tell me about a time when being a civilian faculty member was important in your interactions with a cadet(s).
   - Tell me about a time when being a civilian faculty member led to less successful interactions with a cadet(s).
d. Describe what you see as the importance of having military members as part of the faculty.
   - Tell me about a time when being a military faculty member was important in your interactions with a cadet(s).
   - Tell me about a time when being a military faculty member led to less successful interactions with a cadet(s).

Recruiting Civilians

1. When there are civilian job openings, is there any difficulty in recruiting high-quality candidates?
   a. Why?

Recruiting Military (All questions except question 4 are for military faculty members only)

1. As a military officer, how did you arrive as a faculty member at USAFA?
2. How long will you be a faculty member here?
3. What will likely be your next assignment after USAFA?
4. [All faculty] Are there difficulties in getting military officers assigned to teach at USAFA?
5. What are perceptions in the Air Force about serving as a faculty member at USAFA?

Closing Comments and Thanks

Thank you so much for meeting with us today. The information you provided is critical for our analysis.

APPENDIX C

Overview of Cadet Survey Sample and Methodology

This appendix presents details on the cadet survey sample and survey content.

Survey Sample

We sent an email invitation for participation in an online survey to all cadets at USAFA in the spring of 2011 (4,503 cadets). To help increase the response rate, we sent out several reminder email requests. We also solicited the help of USAFA in advertising the survey to cadets. The Dean of Faculty included an announcement about participation in the survey in her weekly email to cadets, academic faculty made announcements in their classrooms, and the Commandant sent a reminder email on our behalf to all cadets.

A total of 1,642 cadets completed the survey, providing an initial response rate of 36 percent. We then eliminated any problematic responses (i.e., surveys with a large percentage of unanswered questions, completion time of less than seven minutes, incorrect response to a screening question),[1] which reduced the sample size to 859 participants for a final response rate of 19 percent. The final sample of cadets in terms of class year was 27 percent class of 2014, 28 percent class of 2013, 28 percent class of 2012, and 17 percent class of 2011. In terms

[1] One item was purposely designed to verify cadet engagement with the survey and detect possible random responses by directing respondents to select a specific response.

of major academic division,[2] 1⌧ percent of respondents were engineering majors, 12 percent were basic sciences majors, ⌧ percent were humanities majors, 2⌧ percent were social science majors, 1⌧ percent were interdisciplinary or double majors, and 2⌧ percent were undecided. All cadets in the class of 2⌧1⌧ were coded as undecided because cadets do not select a major until their second year.

Response Weights

The results presented in this report are intended to be representative of the cadet population as a whole. Therefore, we calculated response weights to account for any differences in rates across cadet class year and academic major. Response rates were calculated as follows:

$$\frac{\text{Proportion of the group in the population}}{\text{Proportion of the group in the sample}}.$$

However, given the overall low response rate (⌧⌧ percent), some caution is warranted when considering the generalizability of these results to the larger cadet population. Tables C.1 and C.2 present the population and sample percentages for class year and major academic division.

Table C.1
Survey Sample, by Class Year

Cadet Class Year	Population Proportion (%)	Sample Proportion (%)
2011	23	17
2012	25	28
2013	26	28
2014	26	27

[2] These categories represent broader academic divisions that encompass specific academic majors, such as biology, chemistry, and electrical engineering.

Table C.2
Survey Sample, by Major Academic Division

Major Academic Division	Population Proportion (%)	Sample Proportion (%)
Engineering	19	17
Basic sciences	10	12
Humanities	5	7
Social sciences	24	27
Interdisciplinary	16	10
Undecided	27	27

NOTE: All cadets in the class of 2014 were coded as undecided because cadets do not declare their major in the first year. Cadets who reported having a double major were included in the interdisciplinary category.

Throughout this report, where relevant, we also present results for the class of 2011 only, given that cadets in this class year had the most exposure to both military and civilian faculty members at the time of our study. Cadets in the earlier years generally have a high load of introductory core classes taught by junior rotating military faculty. In contrast, senior USAFA cadets are generally completing their upper-level academic major classes, typically taught by civilian instructors or non-rotational military faculty members with higher advanced degrees. With this different exposure, cadets in the senior class at the time of the survey (the class of 2011) might have different perceptions of the influence of different USAFA academic faculty groups.

Survey Content

The survey focused on the extent to which cadets perceived interactions with the following four USAFA groups influencing key aspects of their development:

1. academic civilian faculty
2. academic civilian faculty with prior service experience

3. academic active-duty military faculty
4. commandant staff (i.e., AOCs and AMTs).

Given the distinction often made between civilians with prior service experience and civilians with no prior service experience, we thought it was important to see whether cadets perceived these civilian groups as having different degrees of influence on various aspects of their development. In addition, as a point of comparison with active-duty military faculty we also included members of the commandant's staff (AOCs and AMTs), who are active-duty military personnel in charge of military training at USAFA.[3]

In exploring how the USAFA cadet population perceived the influence of different faculty groups with regard to learning and development, our survey focused primarily on the areas of cadet learning and development that are specifically stressed in HQ USAFA Pamphlet 36-3527, *The Officer Development System: Developing Leaders of Character*. The pamphlet describes the purpose and structure of the Officer Development System, which serves as the overarching doctrinal framework for the systematic development of USAFA cadets and details the many aspects of cadet learning and development included in the system.

Obviously, our survey was not able to measure all the potential ways that faculty members could affect cadets, but we believe that the results provide insight into several critical topic areas that are relevant to this research and help confirm some of the different roles that faculty play in helping USAFA achieve its mission. We were also able to examine the impact of faculty on cadet's development in other parts of this research, such as potential differences in teaching effectiveness.

We assessed the impact of the four USAFA groups on the following three outcomes:

- learning Air Force core values
- leadership development
- development of intellectual skills.

[3] To focus responses on academic faculty only, the survey explicitly directed that athletic department faculty should not be included in any of these groups.

We also examined potential differences in the following key faculty roles identified in our focus groups:

- perceived academic depth of knowledge
- ability to connect class material to the operational Air Force
- ability to provide career advice.

To avoid any potential wording bias in a single item, we assessed each of the above constructs with multiple items. For each item, we asked cadets to rate the extent to which their interactions with each of the four groups contributed to their learning or development using a five-point response scale (1 = "to no extent"; 5 = "to a great extent"). We then averaged the item responses to create a single scale score representing the influence of the four groups on each construct. Before administration, we pilot tested the survey and all items with a handful of USAFA graduates who are now doctoral students at the Pardee RAND Graduate School. Based on their input, we revised the survey items to produce the final list of items for each construct, presented below.

Air Force Core Values

To what extent have your interactions with the following groups contributed to your

1. learning how to act in accordance with the Air Force core value of Integrity First?
2. learning how to act in accordance with the Air Force core value of Service Before Self?
3. learning how to act in accordance with the Air Force core value of Excellence in All We Do?

Personal Leadership

To what extent have your interactions with the following groups contributed to your

1. learning to become a good follower?
2. understanding of how to improve as a cadet?
3. learning the importance of complying with the intent of policies?
4. learning the techniques of being a good leader?
5. learning how to set an example of professionalism to others?

Interpersonal Leadership

To what extent have your interactions with the following groups contributed to your

1. learning how to communicate effectively with others?
2. learning how to be a coach to other cadets?
3. learning the importance of mutual respect in your interactions with others?
4. learning the importance of fairness in your interactions with others?
5. learning the importance of ensuring your fellow cadets' well-being?

Team Leadership

To what extent have your interactions with the following groups contributed to your

1. learning how to effectively lead a team?
2. learning how to get team members to work together?
3. learning how to build a positive team identity?
4. learning how to get team members to use their different skills in support of a common goal?
5. learning how to make decisions that are in the best interest of the entire team?

Organizational Leadership

To what extent have your interactions with the following groups contributed to your

1. learning how to effectively lead an organization?
2. learning how to motivate all members of an organization to perform to the best of their ability?
3. learning how to create an environment that allows all members of an organization to reach their full potential?
4. learning how to coordinate the efforts of several different groups toward broader organizational goals?

Ability to Connect the Classroom to the Air Force

To what extent do the following groups

1. use relevant Air Force examples to explain key concepts in class?
2. have knowledge of recent Air Force situations that relate to course content?

Career Advice

To what extent have your interactions with the following groups contributed to your

1. knowledge of different career options within the Air Force?
2. knowledge of the types of assignments you would receive with different Air Force Specialty Codes (AFSCs)?
3. knowledge of the kinds of training you would experience with different Air Force Specialty Codes (AFSCs)?
4. intended (or awarded) choice of Air Force Specialty Codes (AFSCs)?

Intellectual Skill Development

To what extent have your interactions with the following groups contributed to your

1. learning the skills to effectively analyze quantitative problems?
2. learning the skills to effectively use different sources of information to solve a problem?
3. learning the skills to communicate effectively with others?
4. learning the skills to critically analyze a problem?
5. learning the skills to make effective decisions?

Faculty Academic Depth of Knowledge

During class time, to what extent do the follow groups

1. discuss their knowledge of recent research related to the class material?
2. discuss how the material being taught in class is applicable to situations beyond the military context?
3. discuss the latest developments in the academic subject being taught in class?

Importance of Faculty Characteristics When Teaching a Class

Please rank order the importance of the following faculty characteristics to you when taking a course at USAFA (1 = the most important characteristic and 5 = the least important characteristic).

1. how knowledgeable the instructor is of the course topic
2. the extent to which the instructor is a good military role model
3. the extent to which the instructor teaches the material in a way that will be useful to your future military career
4. the extent to which the instructor discusses the applications of course material beyond the military
5. the teaching experience of the instructor.

APPENDIX D

Additional Information on Relative Teaching Effectiveness Analyses

This appendix presents more detailed information about the mixed-effects models that we used in our analysis of relative teaching effectiveness, as well as data on the randomized assignment of students to sections in a given course. Here, we also provide more information about the data used in our analysis. For each semester and year of a given course, we provide tables showing the total student sample size, the total number of sections, and the total number of each type of faculty.

Mixed-Effects Models

This section provides more information on the mixed-effects models used in our analysis to examine the extent to which military and civilian faculty members have a different impact on student achievement at USAFA. We constructed separate mixed-effects models for the value-added of introductory course instructors on introductory course student achievement and for the value-added of introductory course instructors on follow-on course student achievement. Normalized course scores serve as measures of student achievement in this context.

For a set of students who are indexed by $i = 1,\ldots,N$, the model for the normalized introductory course student grade $Y^{1}_{its^{1}j^{1}}$ of student i in semester-year t with contemporaneous course instructor j^{1} in introductory course section s^{1} was as follows:

$$Y^1_{its^1j^1} = \lambda^1_{j^1} + \eta^1_{tj^1} + \delta^1_{tj^1s^1} + X_{its^1}\beta^1 + X_{j^1} + \varepsilon_{itj^1s^1},$$

where X_{its^1} are regressors, including an intercept, student-level characteristics, and section-level mean characteristics respective to the introductory course section, and X_{j^1} are dummy variables relative to contemporaneous course professor types (i.e., civilian, civilian with prior service experience, and active-duty military). The other parameters in the model are $\lambda^1_{j^1}$, random contemporaneous course instructor-specific effects; $\eta^1_{tj^1}$, random semester-year within contemporaneous course instructor-specific effects; $\delta^1_{tj^1s^1}$, random section within a semester-year within contemporaneous course instructor-specific effects; and $\varepsilon_{itj^1s^1}$, an idiosyncratic error.

For a set of students who are indexed by $i = 1,\ldots,N$, the model for the normalized follow-on course student grade of $Y^2_{it^1t^2j^1j^2s^1s^2}$ of student i in follow-on course semester year t^2 with follow-on course instructor j^2 in follow-on course section s^2, and introductory course professor j^1 in introductory course section s^1 during semester year t^1 was as follows:

$$Y^2_{it^1t^2j^1j^2s^1s^2} = \lambda^2_{j^1} + \eta^2_{t^1j^1} + \delta^2_{t^1j^1s^1} + \upsilon_{t^2s^2} + X_{it^2s^2}\beta^2 + X_{j^1}\beta^2 + \varepsilon_{it^1t^2j^1j^2s^1s^2},$$

where $X_{it^2s^2}$ are regressors, including an intercept and student-level characteristics respective to the follow-on course section, and X_{j^1} are the dummy variables respective to the introductory course instructor types. The other parameters in the model are $\lambda^2_{j^1}$, random introductory course instructor-specific effects; $\eta^2_{t^1j^1}$, random semester-year within introductory instructor-specific effects; and $\delta^2_{t^1j^1s^1}$, random section within semester-year within introductory instructor-specific effects. An additional parameter, $\upsilon_{t^2s^2}$, is a dummy variable for follow-on course sections by semester-year. We included this dummy variable in the model to control for the clustering of students into follow-on course sections.[1] The idiosyncratic error is $\varepsilon_{it^1t^2j^1j^2s^1s^2}$.

---

1 While we specified that the dummy variables be included for each unique follow-on section by semester-year, the software that we used to estimate the mixed-effects models

While the data showed no large-scale systematic variation in student or average section-level characteristics across the different types of faculty in the courses examined, there were a few instances in which average student- and section-level characteristics exhibited statistically significant differences across the three different types of faculty instructing a single course. To control for these instances in which the randomization may have unintentionally yielded small differences in student- and average section-level characteristics across the different faculty types teaching a given course, we included student- and section-level average covariates in the mixed-effects models.

Validating Random Assignments

To examine whether the purported randomized assignment of students to sections of a given course holds, we regressed student and section averaged pretreatment SAT and academic composite scores on the faculty type indicators in the respective course sections. These models used random effects to control for various levels as employed in the primary models used to describe student grades.

For each course, we ran separate random-effects models with average section-level SAT verbal score, average section-level SAT math score, section-level academic composite average, student-level SAT verbal score, student-level SAT math score, and student-level academic composite as dependent variables. We separately regressed the follow-on student- and section-level covariates on the respective introductory course section faculty types and contemporaneous follow-on section faculty types to examine the random assignment to follow-on sections based on introductory and follow-on course faculty types, respectively.

excluded some of these follow-on section dummy variables due to issues of collinearity. For instance, there were 366 different sections of the follow-on math course across the years covered in our data, but the software excluded ten follow-on section dummy variables due to collinearity. For the follow-on chemistry course, there were 440 different follow-on sections over the years covered in the data, but our software omitted 25 sections from the mixed-effects model. Finally, there were 583 sections of the follow-on history courses, and the software omitted 33 dummy variables in the mixed-effects model estimation for these courses.

The resulting coefficients yielded by these models are displayed in Tables D.1–D.8.

According to these results, it appears that the random assignment of students to sections may, in some instances, have resulted in some small differences in the section- and student-level averages among the sections taught by the different faculty types. In addition, while there are a few statistically significant differences, it is difficult to conclude that they are practically significant. For instance, the results in Table D.5 show that students in follow-on math sections who had a prior-service civilian for their introductory math course had section-level SAT verbal scores that were, on average, 7.28 points lower than those of students in follow-on math course sections who had active-duty military instructors for their introductory math course. At the same time, the average SAT verbal average for those sections taught by active-duty military personnel was 620.1, so this difference is fairly small overall. Nevertheless, some of the demonstrated differences in section averages and student-level characteristics in sections taught by different faculty types indicate that these section- and student-level covariates should be used in the random-effects models on student performance to control for these differences.

Table D.1
Check for Randomized Student Assignment to Introductory Math Course Sections Based on Introductory Math Course Faculty Type

Variable	Section SAT Verbal	Section SAT Math	Section Academic Composite	SAT Math	SAT Verbal	Academic Composite
Civilian vs. military	1.47	2.14	–0.01	2.14	1.88	–0.02
Prior-service civilian vs. military	–5.66	–2.26	–0.04	–2.46	–5.56	–0.06

Table D.2
Check for Randomized Student Assignment to Introductory Chemistry Course Sections Based on Introductory Chemistry Course Faculty Type

Variable	Section SAT Verbal	Section SAT Math	Section Academic Composite	SAT Math	SAT Verbal	Academic Composite
Civilian vs. military	–2.12	Did not converge	–0.12	–1.60	–2.20	–0.11
Prior-service civilian vs. military	–5.97	Did not converge	0.17	–5.90	–5.90	0.17

Table D.3
Check for Randomized Student Assignment to Introductory Physics Course Sections Based on Introductory Physics Course Faculty Type

Explanatory Variable	Section SAT Verbal	Section SAT Math	Section Academic Composite	SAT Math	SAT Verbal	Academic Composite
Civilian vs. military	−0.04	4.27	0.11	4.41	−0.01	0.11
Prior-service civilian vs. military	−6.7	−1.75	−0.029	−1.64	−6.21	−0.03

Table D.4
Check for Randomized Student Assignment to Introductory History Course Sections Based on Introductory History Course Faculty Type

Variable	Section SAT Verbal	Section SAT Math	Section Academic Composite	SAT Math	SAT Verbal	Academic Composite
Civilian vs. military	−0.29	2.74	0.14	2.80	−0.32	0.15
Prior-service civilian vs. military	5.96	9.56	0.22	9.60*	5.70	0.22

Table D.5
Check for Randomized Student Assignment to Follow-On Math Course Sections Based on Introductory Math Course Faculty Type

Explanatory Variable	Section SAT Verbal	Section SAT Math	Section Academic Composite	SAT Math	SAT Verbal	Academic Composite
Civilian vs. military	1.65	6.17	0.13	4.06	Did not converge	0.01
Prior-service civilian vs. military	–7.28*	–1.46	–0.06	–1.83	Did not converge	–0.096

NOTE: * $p \leq 0.05$.

Table D.6
Check for Randomized Student Assignment to Follow-On Chemistry Course Sections Based on Introductory Chemistry Course Faculty Type

Explanatory Variable	Section SAT Verbal	Section SAT Math	Section Academic Composite	SAT Math	SAT Verbal	Academic Composite
Civilian vs. military	–0.88	Did not converge	–0.09	–2.10	–1.48	–0.17
Prior-service civilian vs. military	2.87	Did not converge	0.29**	–8.80	–3.81	0.02

NOTE: ** $p \leq 0.01$.

Table D.7
Check for Randomized Student Assignment to Follow-On Physics Course Sections Based on Introductory Physics Course Faculty Type

Explanatory Variable	Section SAT Verbal	Section SAT Math	Section Academic Composite	SAT Math	SAT Verbal	Academic Composite
Civilian vs. military	−1.4	0.21	0.11	2.48	−1.05	0.07
Prior-service civilian vs. military	−0.87	−1.78	−0.02	−1.61	−4.44	−0.07

Table D.8
Check for Randomized Student Assignment to Follow-On History Course Sections Based on Introductory History Course Faculty Type

Explanatory Variable	Section SAT Verbal	Section SAT Math	Section Academic Composite	SAT Math	SAT Verbal	Academic Composite
Civilian vs. military	−2.17	−2.39	−0.05	3.32	−2.38	0.04
Prior-service civilian vs. military	−0.69	1.14	−0.07	1.09	3.30	−0.26

Course Data, by Semester-Year

This section presents data on the total student sample size, the total number of sections, and the total number of faculty of each category for each course-year of each course. Because this analysis looked at the relationship between introductory course student performance and contemporaneous faculty type, follow-on course student performance and introductory faculty type, and follow-on course student performance and follow-on faculty type in five subject areas, Tables D.9–D.24 provide data respective to these analyzed relationships.

Table D.9
Introductory Math Course Faculty Data for Value-Added of Introductory Course Faculty in Contemporaneous Course, by Faculty Type

	Number of Faculty				
Introductory Course Semester	Civilian	Prior-Service Civilian	Military	Missing	Total
Fall 1997	1	1	7	1	10
Spring 1998	0	0	3	0	3
Fall 1998	2	0	9	0	11
Spring 1999	0	0	4	0	4
Fall 1999	0	0	10	0	10
Spring 2000	0	0	3	0	3
Fall 2000	0	0	11	0	11
Spring 2001	0	1	3	0	4
Fall 2001	0	2	8	0	10
Spring 2002	1	0	2	1	4
Fall 2002	3	1	5	0	9
Spring 2003	1	0	5	0	6
Fall 2003	1	1	6	0	8
Spring 2004	0	0	2	0	2
Fall 2004	1	0	9	0	10
Spring 2005	0	0	2	0	2
Fall 2005	1	0	11	0	12
Spring 2006	0	0	2	0	2
Fall 2006	1	1	11	0	13
Spring 2007	1	0	2	0	3
Total	13	7	115	2	137

Table D.10
Introductory Math Course Section and Student Data for Value-Added of Introductory Course Faculty in Contemporaneous Course

Introductory Course Semester	Number of Sections	Number of Students
Fall 1997	25	461
Spring 1998	7	100
Fall 1998	32	532
Spring 1999	7	99
Fall 1999	28	532
Spring 2000	8	150
Fall 2000	27	571
Spring 2001	9	173
Fall 2001	28	528
Spring 2002	10	193
Fall 2002	20	338
Spring 2003	15	278
Fall 2003	28	542
Spring 2004	4	71
Fall 2004	30	521
Spring 2005	5	83
Fall 2005	38	766
Spring 2006	4	67
Fall 2006	42	788
Spring 2007	6	101
Total	373	6,894

Table D.11
Introductory Chemistry Course Faculty Data for Value-Added of Introductory Course Faculty in Contemporaneous Course, by Faculty Type

	Number of Faculty				
Introductory Course Semester	Civilian	Prior-Service Civilian	Military	Missing	Total
Fall 1997	7	0	9	0	16
Fall 1998	2	0	13	0	15
Fall 1999	5	0	17	0	22
Fall 2000	5	1	16	0	22
Fall 2001	6	1	13	1	21
Fall 2002	4	1	14	0	19
Fall 2003	3	0	19	0	22
Fall 2004	3	3	18	0	24
Fall 2005	5	4	15	0	24
Fall 2006	6	2	15	0	23
Total	46	12	149	1	208

Table D.12
Introductory Chemistry Course Section and Student Data for Value-Added of Introductory Course Faculty in Contemporaneous Course

Introductory Course Semester	Number of Sections	Number of Students
Fall 1997	38	765
Fall 1998	42	892
Fall 1999	50	987
Fall 2000	50	1073
Fall 2001	47	994
Fall 2002	48	917
Fall 2003	48	1,024
Fall 2004	50	1,070
Fall 2005	47	1,085
Fall 2006	45	1,035
Total	465	9,842

Table D.13
Introductory Physics Course Faculty Data for Value-Added of Introductory Course Faculty in Contemporaneous Course, by Faculty Type

	Number of Faculty				
Introductory Course Semester	Civilian	Prior-Service Civilian	Military	Missing	Total
Fall 1997	2	0	7	0	9
Spring 1998	1	1	9	0	11
Fall 1998	0	1	8	1	10
Spring 1999	2	1	10	1	14
Fall 1999	1	4	4	0	9
Spring 2000	4	3	7	0	14
Fall 2000	3	1	8	0	12
Spring 2001	4	1	9	0	14
Fall 2001	3	2	6	1	12
Spring 2002	3	2	6	0	11
Fall 2002	3	1	5	0	9
Spring 2003	4	1	4	0	9
Fall 2003	1	2	7	0	10
Spring 2004	1	4	10	0	15
Fall 2004	2	1	6	1	10
Spring 2005	2	6	7	1	16
Fall 2005	1	1	7	0	9
Spring 2006	1	3	6	0	10
Fall 2006	2	0	10	0	12
Spring 2007	3	1	7	0	11
Total	43	36	143	5	227

Table D.14
Introductory Physics Course Section and Student Data for Value-Added of Introductory Course Faculty in Contemporaneous Course

Introductory Course Semester	Number of Sections	Number of Students
Fall 1997	25	461
Spring 1998	22	467
Fall 1998	25	430
Spring 1999	27	534
Fall 1999	24	429
Spring 2000	30	603
Fall 2000	24	523
Spring 2001	26	578
Fall 2001	26	505
Spring 2002	25	514
Fall 2002	20	507
Spring 2003	16	455
Fall 2003	22	492
Spring 2004	26	592
Fall 2004	26	509
Spring 2005	28	598
Fall 2005	24	532
Spring 2006	26	485
Fall 2006	30	663
Spring 2007	23	551
Total	495	10,428

Table D.15
Introductory History Course Faculty Data for Value-Added of Introductory Course Faculty in Contemporaneous Course, by Faculty Type

	Number of Faculty				
Introductory Course Semester	Civilian	Prior-Service Civilian	Military	Missing	Total
Fall 1997	3	0	9	0	12
Spring 1998	3	0	8	0	11
Fall 1998	2	0	12	0	14
Spring 1999	2	0	8	0	10
Fall 1999	1	1	10	0	12
Spring 2000	1	0	9	1	11
Fall 2000	2	0	8	1	11
Spring 2001	2	0	9	0	11
Fall 2001	1	0	9	0	10
Spring 2002	3	0	6	1	10
Fall 2002	2	1	8	1	12
Spring 2003	3	1	8	1	13
Fall 2003	2	1	5	1	9
Spring 2004	3	0	8	1	12
Fall 2004	1	0	9	0	10
Spring 2005	0	0	11	2	13
Fall 2005	2	0	9	0	11
Spring 2006	1	0	9	0	10
Fall 2006	3	0	9	0	12
Spring 2007	1	1	6	0	8
Total	38	5	170	9	222

Table D.16
Introductory History Course Section and Student Data for Value-Added of Introductory Course Faculty in Contemporaneous Course

Introductory Course Semester	Number of Sections	Number of Students
Fall 1997	37	602
Spring 1998	26	383
Fall 1998	34	622
Spring 1999	24	427
Fall 1999	34	667
Spring 2000	26	439
Fall 2000	31	604
Spring 2001	33	521
Fall 2001	33	659
Spring 2002	26	454
Fall 2002	31	591
Spring 2003	29	481
Fall 2003	28	569
Spring 2004	29	496
Fall 2004	34	672
Spring 2005	34	645
Fall 2005	32	646
Spring 2006	27	564
Fall 2006	32	666
Spring 2007	24	491
Total	604	11,199

Table D.17
Introductory Math Course Faculty Data for Value-Added of Introductory Course Faculty in Follow-On Course, by Faculty Type

	Number of Faculty				
Introductory Course Semester	Civilian	Prior-Service Civilian	Military	Missing	Total
Fall 1997	1	1	7	1	10
Spring 1998	0	0	3	0	3
Fall 1998	2	0	9	0	11
Spring 1999	0	0	4	0	4
Fall 1999	0	0	10	0	10
Spring 2000	0	0	3	0	3
Fall 2000	0	0	11	0	11
Spring 2001	0	1	3	0	4
Fall 2001	0	2	8	0	10
Spring 2002	1	0	3	0	4
Fall 2002	3	1	5	0	9
Spring 2003	1	0	5	0	6
Fall 2003	1	1	6	0	8
Spring 2004	0	0	2	0	2
Fall 2004	1	0	9	0	10
Spring 2005	0	0	2	0	2
Fall 2005	1	0	11	0	12
Spring 2006	0	0	2	0	2
Fall 2006	1	1	11	0	13
Total	12	7	114	1	134

Table D.18
Introductory Math Course Section and Student Data for Value-Added of Introductory Course Faculty in Follow-On Course

Introductory Course Semester	Number of Sections	Number of Students
Fall 1997	25	458
Spring 1998	7	90
Fall 1998	32	518
Spring 1999	7	85
Fall 1999	28	530
Spring 2000	7	112
Fall 2000	27	532
Spring 2001	9	148
Fall 2001	28	501
Spring 2002	10	163
Fall 2002	20	315
Spring 2003	15	229
Fall 2003	28	530
Spring 2004	4	60
Fall 2004	29	481
Spring 2005	5	64
Fall 2005	37	703
Spring 2006	4	58
Fall 2006	42	689
Missing	0	448
Total	364	6,714

Table D.19
Introductory Chemistry Course Faculty Data for Value-Added of Introductory Course Faculty in Follow-On Course, by Faculty Type

	Number of Faculty				
Introductory Course Semester	Civilian	Prior-Service Civilian	Military	Missing	Total
Fall 1997	7	1	10	0	18
Spring 1998	0	0	1	0	1
Fall 1998	4	0	13	0	17
Spring 1999	0	0	1	0	1
Fall 1999	5	0	20	0	25
Fall 2000	5	1	18	0	24
Fall 2001	6	1	15	1	23
Fall 2002	5	1	15	0	21
Fall 2003	3	0	19	0	22
Fall 2004	3	3	19	0	25
Fall 2005	5	4	16	0	25
Fall 2006	6	3	15	0	24
Total	49	14	162	1	226

Table D.20
Introductory Chemistry Course Section and Student Data for Value-Added of Introductory Course Faculty in Follow-On Course

Introductory Course Semester	Number of Sections	Number of Students
Fall 1997	42	711
Spring 1998	1	1
Fall 1998	44	805
Spring 1999	1	1
Fall 1999	53	894
Fall 2000	53	964
Fall 2001	50	901
Fall 2002	52	804
Fall 2003	49	918
Fall 2004	51	907
Fall 2005	51	939
Fall 2006	49	877
Missing	0	50
Total	496	8,772

Table D.21
Introductory Physics Course Faculty Data for Value-Added of Introductory Course Faculty in Follow-On Course, by Faculty Type

	Number of Faculty				
Introductory Course Semester	Civilian	Prior-Service Civilian	Military	Missing	Total
Fall 1997	2	0	7	0	9
Spring 1998	1	1	9	0	11
Fall 1998	0	1	8	1	10
Spring 1999	2	1	10	1	14
Fall 1999	1	4	4	0	9
Spring 2000	4	3	7	0	14
Fall 2000	3	1	8	0	12
Spring 2001	4	1	9	0	14
Fall 2001	3	2	6	1	12
Spring 2002	3	2	6	0	11
Fall 2002	3	1	5	0	9
Spring 2003	4	1	4	0	9
Fall 2003	1	2	7	0	10
Spring 2004	1	4	10	0	15
Fall 2004	2	1	6	1	10
Spring 2005	2	6	7	1	16
Fall 2005	1	1	7	0	9
Spring 2006	1	3	6	0	10
Fall 2006	2	0	10	0	12
Total	40	35	136	5	216

Table D.22
Introductory Physics Course Section and Student Data for Value-Added of Introductory Course Faculty in Follow-On Course

Introductory Course Semester	Number of Sections	Number of Students
Fall 1997	24	365
Spring 1998	21	403
Fall 1998	25	413
Spring 1999	27	510
Fall 1999	24	414
Spring 2000	30	575
Fall 2000	23	480
Spring 2001	26	538
Fall 2001	26	459
Spring 2002	25	477
Fall 2002	20	458
Spring 2003	16	427
Fall 2003	22	464
Spring 2004	26	541
Fall 2004	26	480
Spring 2005	28	565
Fall 2005	24	488
Spring 2006	26	433
Fall 2006	30	576
Missing	0	885
Total	469	9,951

Table D.23
Introductory History Course Faculty Data for Value-Added of Introductory Course Faculty in Follow-On Course, by Faculty Type

	Number of Faculty				
Introductory Course Semester	Civilian	Prior-Service Civilian	Military	Missing	Total
Fall 1997	3	0	9	0	12
Spring 1998	3	0	8	0	11
Fall 1998	2	0	12	0	14
Spring 1999	2	0	8	0	10
Fall 1999	1	1	10	0	12
Spring 2000	1	0	9	1	11
Fall 2000	2	0	8	1	11
Spring 2001	2	0	9	0	11
Fall 2001	1	0	9	0	10
Spring 2002	3	0	6	1	10
Fall 2002	2	1	8	1	12
Spring 2003	3	1	8	1	13
Fall 2003	2	1	5	1	9
Spring 2004	3	0	8	1	12
Fall 2004	1	0	9	0	10
Spring 2005	0	0	11	2	13
Fall 2005	2	0	9	0	11
Spring 2006	1	0	9	0	10
Fall 2006	3	0	9	0	12
Spring 2007	0	0	1	0	1
Total	37	4	165	9	215

Table D.24
Introductory History Course Section and Student Data for Value-Added of Introductory Course Faculty in Follow-On Course

Introductory Course Semester	Number of Sections	Number of Students
Fall 1997	37	578
Spring 1998	26	370
Fall 1998	34	572
Spring 1999	24	405
Fall 1999	34	647
Spring 2000	26	423
Fall 2000	31	546
Spring 2001	33	475
Fall 2001	33	580
Spring 2002	26	411
Fall 2002	31	510
Spring 2003	29	431
Fall 2003	28	509
Spring 2004	29	441
Fall 2004	34	577
Spring 2005	34	580
Fall 2005	32	436
Spring 2006	27	458
Fall 2006	28	97
Spring 2007	1	2
Missing	0	936
Total	577	9,984

APPENDIX E

Comparison with Carrell and West's Value-Added Approach

This appendix presents greater detail on the differences between our analysis and a 2010 study by Scott Carrell and James West titled "Does Professor Quality Matter? Evidence from Random Assignment of Students to Professors," published in the [illegible].

In their study, Carrell and West explored the relationship between the characteristics of introductory math course instructors at [illegible] and student achievement in the introductory math course and in a set of follow-on courses for which the introductory math course served as a prerequisite. From a data set of students who attended [illegible] from the fall of 2[illegible] through the spring of 2[illegible], the authors used a two-stage procedure to estimate the impact of professors' characteristics on students' standardized scores. The authors first employed random-effects models to estimate parameters for instructor value-added on student performance, referred to as Bayesian shrinkage estimates, while controlling for student-specific characteristics, mean peer characteristics, and unobserved mean differences in academic achievement or grading standards across time.

The random-effects models that Carrell and West employed for introductory course grades and follow-on course grades are described below using the authors' notation. Carrell and West used a superscript 1 to denote an introductory course section and a superscript 2 to denote a follow-on course section. For a set of students indexed by $i = 1,\ldots,N$, sections $s^1 \in \mathbb{S}$ of the introductory course, introductory course instructors indexed by $j^1 = 1,\ldots,j$, sections $s^2 \in \mathbb{S}$ of the follow-on course, and follow-on course instructors indexed by $j^2 = 1,\ldots,j$, the model for the normalized introductory math course student performance was specified as

$$Y^1_{itj^1j^2s^1s^2} = X_{its^1}\beta^1 + \gamma^1_t + \lambda^1_{j^1} + \lambda^1_{j^2} + \xi^1_{ts^1} + \xi^1_{ts^2} + \varepsilon^1_{itj^1j^2s^1s^2},$$

where $Y^1_{itj^1j^2s^1s^2}$ is the normalized percentage of introductory course points earned by student i in semester-year t with introductory course instructor j^1 in introductory course section s^1 and follow-on course instructor j^2 in follow-on course section s^2. Vectors of student-specific and classroom mean peer characteristics relevant to section s^1 in semester-year t are contained in X_{its^1}. Carrell and West controlled for "unobserved mean differences in academic achievement or grading standards across time" in the course by semester intercept, γ^1_t.[1]

In their model of introductory course student performance, Carrell and West included random effects relative to specific instructors and specific sections. Relevant to the model for introductory math course student performance, $\lambda^1_{j^1}$ measures the value-added of introductory course instructor j^1 in the contemporaneous introductory course, and $\lambda^1_{j^2}$ measures the value-added of follow-on course instructor j^2 in the introductory course.[2]

Carrell and West included section-specific random effects to measure "classroom-level common shocks that are independent across professors j and time t."[3] Relevant to the model on introductory math course student performance, $\xi^1_{ts^1}$ measures the introductory course section-specific shock in the contemporaneous introductory course, and $\xi^1_{ts^2}$ measures the follow-on course section-specific common shock in the introductory course. Carrell and West included $\lambda^1_{j^2}$ and $\xi^1_{ts^2}$ as an additional means of verifying the randomization of students to sections. The final term, $\varepsilon^1_{itj^1j^2s^1s^2}$, is the student-specific stochastic error term in the introductory course.

---

1 Carrell and West, 2010, p. 420.

2 The inclusion of $\lambda^1_{j^2}$ allows for a second test of randomized assignment.

3 Carrell and West, 2010, p. 420.

Using the same indexing format, Carrell and West's model for follow-on math course student performance was specified as

$$Y^{2}_{itj^1j^2s^1s^2} = X_{its^2}\beta^2 + \gamma^2_t + \lambda^2_{j^2} + \lambda^2_{j^1} + \xi^2_{ts^2} + \xi^2_{ts^1} + \varepsilon^2_{itj^1j^2s^1s^2},$$

where $Y^{2}_{itj^1j^2s^1s^2}$ is the normalized percentage of follow-on course points earned by student i in semester-year t with introductory course instructor j^1 in introductory course section s^1 and follow-on course instructor j^2 in follow-on course section s^2. Vectors of student-specific and classroom mean peer characteristics relevant to follow-on course section s^2 in semester-year t are contained in X_{its^2}. Carrell and West controlled for "unobserved mean differences in academic achievement or grading standards across time" in the course by semester intercept γ^1_t. They controlled for "unobserved mean differences in academic achievement or grading standards across time" in the course by semester intercept γ^2_t. The final term, $\varepsilon^2_{itj^1j^2s^1s^2}$, is the student-specific stochastic error term in the follow-on course.

As with the model on introductory course student achievement, Carrell and West included random effects relative to specific instructors and specific sections. They used $\lambda^2_{j^2}$ to measure the value-added of follow-on course instructor j^2 in the contemporaneous follow-on course. They used $\lambda^2_{j^1}$ to measure the value-added of introductory course professor j^1 in the follow-on course. With regard to the section-specific random effects, $\xi^2_{ts^2}$ measures the follow-on course section-specific shock in the contemporaneous follow-on course, and $\xi^2_{ts^1}$ measures the introductory course section-specific common shock in the follow-on course.

Although Carrell and West's "professor value-added model estimates the total variance in professor inputs (observed and unobserved) in student academic achievement,"[4] they state that "one disadvantage of [their] professor value-added model is that it is unable to measure which observable professor characteristics actually predict student

4 Carrell and West, 2010, p. 419.

achievement."[5] Carrell and West also state that their "model provides little or no information to administrators wishing to improve future hiring practices";[6] they regress the normalized Bayesian shrinkage estimates of professor value-added on observable professor characteristics as an additional step to provide this information.

After estimating the two random-effects models presented here, Carrel and West conducted a series of bivariate regressions, in which the parameters for estimating introductory math course instructor value-added are regressed on professor-observable characteristics. Carrell and West use these bivariate regressions to determine which observable instructor characteristics are correlated with instructor value-added. The results of these regressions using observable instructor characteristics are reproduced in Table E.1. Each row of the table represents a separate bivariate regression with a unique introductory math course faculty attribute serving as the explanatory variable. The first column in Table E.1 shows the resulting coefficients from separate regressions in which the introductory math course instructor's value-added in the contemporaneous math course, $\lambda^{1}_{j^1}$, is regressed on the respective observable introductory math course instructor characteristic. The second column in Table E.1 shows the resulting coefficients from separate regressions in which the introductory math course instructor's value-added in the follow-on math course, $\lambda^{2}_{j^1}$, is regressed on the respective introductory math course observable professor char-

Table E.1
Observable Instructor Characteristics from Carrell and West (2010)

Professor Observable Characteristics	Introductory Math Course	Follow-on Math Course
Associate/full professor	−0.69*	0.70*
Terminal degree	−0.28	0.38
More than 3 years' teaching experience	−0.79***	0.66***

NOTE: *** $p \leq 0.01$, * $p \leq 0.1$.

[5] Carrell and West, 2010, p. 427.

[6] Carrell and West, 2010, p. 427.

acteristic. In each of these regressions, the Bayesian shrinkage estimates were normalized to have a mean of zero and a variance of 1.

The negative coefficient of –0.69 in the first column for the associate/full professor variable indicates that the Bayesian shrinkage estimates of contemporaneous value-added among associate and full professors are 0.69 standard deviations lower on average than the Bayesian shrinkage estimates of faculty not in the associate or full professor ranks. On the other hand, the positive coefficient of 0.70 in the second column for the associate/full professor variable indicates that the Bayesian shrinkage estimates of follow-on course value-added for associate and full professors are 0.70 standard deviations higher on average than the Bayesian shrinkage estimates of follow-on course value-added for faculty not in the associate or full professor ranks. The other variables exhibit a similar pattern between the introductory and follow-on related courses. Hence, Carrell and West conclude that "less experienced and less qualified professors produce students who perform significantly better in the contemporaneous course being taught, whereas more experienced and highly qualified professors produce students who perform better in the follow-on related curriculum."[7]

In general, civilian faculty are more likely to be full professors, have doctorates, and have more years of teaching experience, so one can extrapolate that civilian faculty are more likely to "produce students who perform better in the follow-on related curriculum." However, Carrell and West did not directly examine the associations between types of faculty and students' performance, which was the central purpose of our research.

Beyond this basic difference in the purpose of our research, there are several additional differences between our analysis and Carrell and West's study. For instance, we used the same data set as Carrell and West to explore the relationships between USAFA professor value-added, observable professor characteristics, and students' professor evaluations, but there are some differences between the actual data samples covered in our analysis and the analysis of Carrell and West. When examining professor value-added, Carrell and West nor-

---

[7] Carrell and West, 2010, p. 429.

malized "the percentage of points earned within a course/semester to have a mean of zero and a standard deviation of one" and used this as the dependent variable for each student-level observation in their random-effects models.[8] We used a different dependent variable, the normalized student grade. For the purpose of computing a given student's overall grade point average, USAFA assigns each student a numeric value that corresponds to his or her earned alphabetical grade in a course. A student earning an alphabetical grade of A, A-, B+, B, B–, C+, C, D, or F in a course will be given a numerical grade value of 4, 3.7, 3.3, 3, 2.7, 2.3, 2, 1, or 0, respectively. We normalized these equivalent numeric grades to have a mean of 0 and a standard deviation of 1 within each course and semester-year.[9]

Differences are also present in the range of years included in the analysis of these dependent variables. In their analysis of the normalized percentage of points earned by students, Carrell and West analyzed data from the fall of 2000 to the spring of 2007. In our analysis of normalized student grades, we included data from the fall of 1997 to the spring of 2007.[10]

A final difference in the data coverage between these two pieces of research pertains to which courses were specifically considered follow-on courses. In their research on introductory math course instructor value-added in follow-on courses, Carrell and West considered multiple "follow-on courses that require introductory calculus as a prerequisite."[11] For each subject area analyzed, we considered only a single follow-on course, germane to the same subject area.

In terms of our analytical approach, we used mixed-effects models to examine the extent to which military and civilian faculty members had a different effect on student achievement at USAFA, but our meth-

---

8 Carrell and West, 2010, p. 414.

9 While Carrell and West used the normalized percentage of points as the dependent variable in their 2010 article, in an earlier National Bureau of Economic Research working paper version, they used the normalized course grade as the dependent variable of interest.

10 In their National Bureau of Economic Research working paper, the normalized grades that Carrell and West analyzed were also from the fall of 1997 to the spring of 2007.

11 Carrell and West, 2010, p. 9.

ods differed from those of Carrell and West in the specific random effects utilized, the exclusion of the observable faculty characteristics of interest to Carrell and West, and the one-step nature of our model estimation procedure.[12]

Specifically, like Carrell and West, we constructed separate mixed-effects models for exploring the value-added of introductory course instructors on introductory course student achievement and for exploring the value-added of introductory course instructors on follow-on course student achievement. We used normalized course scores as measures of student achievement in this context.

As described in Appendix D of this report, for a set of students who are indexed by $i = 1,\ldots,N$, the model for the normalized introductory course student grade $Y^1_{its^1j^1}$ of student i in semester-year t with contemporaneous course professor j^1 in introductory course section s^1 was as follows:

$$Y^1_{its^1j^1} = \lambda^1_{j^1} \square \eta^1_{tj^1} \square \delta^1_{tj^1s^1} \square X_{its^1}\beta^1 \square X_{j^1}\beta^1 \square \varepsilon_{itj^1s^1},$$

where X_{its^1} are regressors, including an intercept, student-level characteristics, and section-level mean characteristics respective to the introductory course section, and X_{j^1} are dummy variables relative to contemporaneous course professor types (i.e., civilian, civilian with prior service experience, and active-duty military). The other parameters in the model are $\lambda^1_{j^1}$, random contemporaneous course instructor-specific effects; η_{tj^1}, random semester-year within contemporaneous course instructor-specific effects; $\delta^1_{tj^1s^1}$, random section within semester-year within contemporaneous course instructor-specific effects; and $\varepsilon_{itj^1s^1}$, an idiosyncratic error.

For a set of students who are indexed by $i = 1,\ldots,N$, the model for the normalized follow-on course student grade of $Y^2_{it^1t^2j^1j^2s^1s^2}$ of student i in follow-on course semester year t^2 with follow-on course professor j^2 in follow-on course section s^2 and introductory course professor j^1 in introductory course section s^1 during semester year t^1 was specified as

12 James West, former professor of economics, USAFA, generously shared these data with us and assisted in the execution of our models.

$$Y^2_{it^1t^2j^1j^2s^1s^2} = \lambda^2_{j^1} + \eta^2_{t^1j^1} + \delta^2_{t^1j^1s^1} + \upsilon_{t^2s^2} + X_{it^2s^2}\beta^2 + X_{j^1}\beta^2 + \varepsilon_{it^1t^2j^1j^2s^1s^2},$$

where $X_{it^2s^2}$ are regressors, including an intercept and student-level characteristics respective to the follow-on course section, and X_{j^1} are the dummy variables respective to the introductory course instructor types. The other parameters in the model are $\lambda^2_{j^1}$, random introductory course instructor-specific effects; $\eta^2_{t^1j^1}$, random semester-year within introductory instructor-specific effects; and $\delta^2_{t^1j^1s^1}$, random section within semester-year within introductory instructor-specific effects. An additional parameter, $\upsilon_{t^2s^2}$, is a dummy variable for follow-on course sections by semester-year. We included this dummy variable in the model to control for the clustering of students into follow-on course sections. The idiosyncratic error is $\varepsilon_{it^1t^2j^1j^2s^1s^2}$.

While the data showed no large-scale systematic variation in student or average section-level characteristics across the different types of faculty in the courses examined, there were a few instances in which average student and section-level characteristics exhibited statistically significant differences across the three different types of faculty instructing a single course. To control for instances in which the randomization may have unintentionally yielded small differences in average student- and section-level characteristics across the different faculty types teaching a given course, we included student- and section-level average covariates in the random-effects models.

One may notice several differences between our mixed-effects models and the random-effects models employed by Carrell and West. The first difference is in the random effects used in our models. We used a triple-nested random-effects structure to account for the hierarchical clustering of faculty within course sections over multiple years. This nested structure adjusts for many possible clustering effects, such as variation in instructor quality over time or variation in instructor quality across different sections in a given semester-year due to variation in classroom dynamics.

A second difference in our employed random-effects models is that they do not contain explanatory variables indicating an instructor's academic rank, teaching experience, or terminal degree attainment—the observable faculty characteristics of interest to Carrell and West. We excluded these additional faculty-level attributes because the point of our analysis was to determine whether the unique faculty types are differentially effective in and of themselves. In other words, we did not want to estimate associations between types of faculty and students' performance while controlling for other faculty characteristics, such as rank, degree, or teaching experience. These characteristics might contribute to differences in the teaching effectiveness of faculty types and thus should not be included as separate explanatory variables in the model; they should instead be absorbed in the faculty type group differences.

The third difference between our mixed-effects models and those employed by Carrell and West involves the number of steps required to complete the analysis. Carrell and West first obtain their Bayesian shrinkage estimates of instructor value-added via their random-effects models and then separately run a series of bivariate regressions with these Bayesian shrinkage estimates as the dependent variable to determine the relationship between observable faculty characteristics and value-added. In our analysis, we determined what effect the different faculty types had on student achievement by directly including these faculty type variables in our estimated mixed-effects models. By directly estimating the associations between faculty types and student performance in one step, we gain greater efficiency in our estimates.

Finally, examining the experience, academic rank, and terminal degree attainment of these different faculty types further informs differences in the conclusions reached by the separate analyses. Civilian faculty tend to have more teaching experience, higher academic rank, and a terminal degree, but not all civilian faculty meet this description. At the same time, while active-duty military personnel tend to have less teaching experience, hold a lower academic rank, and do not usually possess a terminal degree, there are some military faculty members who have similar teaching experience, academic rank, and terminal degree attainment as their civilian faculty peers. Table E.2 shows the percentage of the different introductory math course faculty types with more than three years of teaching experience, high academic rank, and

Table E.2
Characteristics of Introductory Math Course Faculty

Introductory Math Course Faculty Type	Associate or Full Professor (%)	More Than 3 Years' Teaching Experience (%)	Holding Terminal Degree (%)
Civilian (n = 8)	25.0	37.5	75.0
Prior-service civilian (n = 3)	33.3	66.7	100.0
Active-duty military (n = 51)	5.9	15.7	17.6
Total (N = 62)	9.7	21.0	29.0

SOURCE: Data from Carrell and West, 2010.

a terminal degree from the data that Carrell and West reference in their *Journal of Political Economy* article.

Thus, while status as a civilian professor appears to be highly correlated with the observable faculty attributes that Carrell and West examine, this is not a perfect correlation. As a result, the effect of the faculty type characteristics on student-level outcomes in our study does not exactly align with the effect of the observable faculty characteristics on student-level outcomes found by Carrell and West.

In conclusion, on the surface, our results may appear to contradict those of Carrell and West, but these separate analyses cannot be directly compared because of their myriad differences. While we were concerned with whether civilians, civilians with prior service experience, and active-duty military faculty had different degrees of impact on student learning, Carrell and West were concerned with the correlation between the observable faculty characteristics of experience, academic rank, terminal degree attainment, student evaluation ratings, and value added. Additional differences persist in the specific data analyzed, in our use of triple-nested random effects to control for hierarchical clustering, and in the number of modeling steps required to determine the correlation between professor characteristics and value added. These cumulative differences make a simple comparison of our results to those of Carrell and West problematic.

References

Air Force Instruction 36-3501, *Air Force Academy Operations*, April 28, 2008, certified current as of May 3, 2010.

Air Force Instruction 65-503, *US Air Force Cost and Planning Factors*, February 4, 1994.

Born, Brig Gen Dana H., dean of faculty, United States Air Force Academy, *Dean's Response to the Larson Report on the Faculty System at the Air Force Academy*, December 3, 2004.

———, statement before the Subcommittee on Oversight and Investigations, Committee on Armed Services, U.S. House of Representatives, at the hearing "Beyond Service Core Competency: Are Our Junior Officers Prepared for Today's Security Environment?" Washington, D.C., July 15, 2009.

Carrell, Scott, Marianne E. Page, and James E. West, "Sex and Science: How Professor Gender Perpetuates the Gender Gap," *Quarterly Journal of Economics*, Vol. 25, No. 3, August 2010, pp. 1101–1144.

Carrell, Scott, and James West, "Does Professor Quality Matter? Evidence from Random Assignment of Students to Professors," *Journal of Political Economy*, Vol. 118, No. 3, June 2010, pp. 409–432.

Comptroller General of the United States, *Financial Operations of the Five Service Academies*, Washington, D.C.: U.S. General Accounting Office, FPCD-75-117, February 1975a.

———, *Academic and Military Programs of the Five Service Academies*, Washington, D.C.: U.S. General Accounting Office, FPCD-76-8, October 1975b.

Corbin, Juliet M., and Anselm L. Strauss, *Basics of Qualitative Research: Techniques and Procedures for Developing Grounded Theory*, 3rd ed., Thousand Oaks, Calif.: Sage Publications, 2008.

DoD—*See* U.S. Department of Defense.

Gates, Susan M., and Albert A. Robbert, *Comparing the Costs of DoD Military and Civil Service Personnel*, Santa Monica, Calif.: RAND Corporation, MR-980-OSD, 1998. As of July 31, 2012:
http://www.rand.org/pubs/monograph_reports/MR980.html

House Resolution, National Defense Authorization Act for Fiscal Year 1993, 102nd Congress, 1992.

HQ United States Air Force Academy Instruction 36-151, *Permanent Professor*, March 20, 2000.

HQ United States Air Force Academy Instruction 36-3520, *Senior Military Faculty*, March 31, 2010.

HQ United States Air Force Academy Pamphlet 36-3527, *The Officer Development System: Developing Leaders of Character*, August 11, 2008.

Jones, Paul L., director, Manpower Issues, National Security, and International Affairs Division, U.S. General Accounting Office, *Review of the Cost and Operations of DoD's Service Academies*, statement before the Subcommittee on Manpower and Personnel, Committee on Armed Services, U.S. Senate, Washington, D.C.: U.S. General Accounting Office, GAO/T-NSIAD-90-28, April 4, 1990.

Larson, ADM (ret.) Charles R., *Study and Report Related to Permanent Professors at the United States Air Force Academy*, April 2004.

Lovell, John P., *Neither Athens Nor Sparta? The American Service Academies in Transition*, Bloomington, Ind.: Indiana University Press, 1979.

Maze, Rick, "Bill Would Cut Status, Officer Staff at Academies," *Air Force Times*, Vol. 53, No. 11, October 19, 1992, p. 24.

Miles, Mathew B., and A. Michael Huberman, *Qualitative Data Analysis: An Expanded Sourcebook*, 2nd ed., Thousand Oaks, Calif.: Sage Publications, 1994.

Nunnally, Jum C., and Ira H. Bernstein, *Psychometric Theory*, 3rd ed., New York: McGraw-Hill, 1994.

Nussle, Jim, director, Office of Management and Budget, "Update to Civilian Position Full Fringe Benefit Cost Factor, Federal Pay Raise Assumptions, and Inflation Factors used in OMB Circular No. A-76, 'Performance of Commercial Activities,'" memorandum, Washington, D.C.: Office of Management and Budget, M-08-13, March 11, 2008. As of July 31, 2012:
http://www.whitehouse.gov/sites/default/files/omb/assets/omb/memoranda/fy2008/m08-13.pdf

Office of the Assistant Secretary of Defense for Force Management and Personnel, *A Blend of Excellence: Military-Civilian Faculty Mix at the Service Academies*, Washington, D.C., 1993.

Ostroff, Cheri, Angelo J. Kinicki, and Melinda M. Tamkins, "Organizational Culture and Climate," *Handbook of Psychology*, Vol. 12: *Industrial and Organizational Psychology*, Hoboken, N.J.: Wiley, 2003, pp. 565–593.

Roth, John P., deputy comptroller, Office of the Under Secretary of Defense, Comptroller, "FY 2011 Department of Defense (DoD) Military Personnel Composite Standard Pay and Reimbursement Rate," memorandum, March 24, 2010. As of July 31, 2012:
http://comptroller.defense.gov/rates/fy2011/2011_k.pdf

Schwartz, Gen Norton A., Chief of Staff, U.S. Air Force, "Instructor Duty—Building Leaders Is Everybody's Business," memorandum, March 8, 2012.

Secretary of Veterans Affairs, Veterans Benefits Administration, *Servicemembers' and Veterans' Group Life Insurance Handbook*, Washington, D.C., H-29-98-1, revised February 2011. As of July 31, 2012:
http://www.insurance.va.gov/sglisite/handbook/handbook.pdf

Staats, Elmer B., Comptroller General of the United States, *Education: Federal Service Academies*, statement before the Subcommittee on Legislation and National Security, Committee on Government Operations, U.S. House of Representatives, Washington, D.C., March 17, 1976.

U.S. Air Force Academy, *Dean of Faculty Strategic Plan FY 2009–2014*, Colo., undated. As of July 31, 2012:
http://www.usafa.edu/df/data/DFStratPlan14Apr09WEB.PDF

———, *The United States Air Force Academy Outcomes*, Colo., 2009. As of July 31, 2012:
http://www.usafa.edu/df/data/USAFA%20Outcomes.pdf

U.S. Air Force Academy Faculty Operating Instruction 36-179, *Civilian Faculty Sabbatical Program*, December 21, 2010.

U.S. Department of Defense, *Stearns-Eisenhower Report: A Report and Recommendation to the Secretary of Defense by the Service Academy Board*, Washington, D.C., January 1950.

U.S. General Accounting Office, *DoD Service Academies: Improved Cost and Performance Monitoring Needed*, Washington, D.C., GAO-NSIAD-91-79, July 1991.

U.S. House of Representatives, *Another Crossroads? Professional Military Education Two Decades After the Goldwater-Nichols Act and the Skelton Panel*, transcript of hearing before the Subcommittee on Oversight and Investigations, Committee on Armed Services, U.S. House of Representatives, Washington, D.C., April 2010.